MW00333977

No One Stood Up When I Entered The Room

No One Stood Up When I Entered The Room

One Woman's Journey from **COMMAND** to True *LEADERSHIP*

Linda Patten

Dedication

*This book is dedicated to
all the women leaders
past, present, and future
who stepped up,
stepped out, and
owned their leadership
when it was not a balance
of feminine and masculine qualities.*

*They had the courage and
dared to lead*

Also by Linda Patten

The Art of Herding Cats: Leading Teams of Leaders

Anthologies:

Becoming Outrageously Successful: A Woman's Guide to Finding Her Purpose, Fueling Her Passion and Unlocking Her Prosperity

Come Out of Hiding and Shine: An Anthology

Success Secrets for Today's Feminine Entrepreneur: Secrets that Empower Women to Unlimited and Outrageous Success

Women of Courage, Women of Destiny: Moving from Fear to Faith to Freedom

Empowering You, Transforming Lives: Daily Inspiration to Help You Live on Purpose and with Purpose

Experts and Influencers: The Leadership Edition

Contents

Foreword

WHEN I WAS first introduced to Linda Patten by a mentor, I was told she was a dynamic leader and entrepreneur and that, like me, she is a military veteran. I love connecting with other women vets and looked forward to learning more about Linda's experience. In preparation for our first call, I read her book *The Art of Herding Cats: Leading Teams of Leaders,* and found the advice therein to be both easy to read and to apply.

I was thrilled and deeply honored when Linda later asked me to provide the foreword to this book. *No One Stood Up When I Entered the Room: One Woman's Journey from Command to True Leadership* is the story of this remarkable woman's journey to change her early military command leadership style to one that is more pragmatic, inclusive, and collaborative.

But transforming what worked in the military to that which would be effective in the corporate and entrepreneurial worlds wasn't easy for Linda. I related to the challenges she faced as a woman working to make a difference in the very patriarchal military structure that existed in the 70s. Like many women of that era, she thought the way to succeed was to mimic men's rigid leadership style. And that worked great . . . in the military that was structured by men, for men.

But what worked then would prove disastrous for her later. With courage and candor, Linda shares her first clunky attempts to lead corporate teams by trying to command their attention and loyalty, and her attempts to find a more effective leadership style.

Linda learned—and proposes in this book—a new type of leadership, one based on influence rather than command, and trust rather than control. One that appreciates the value of feminine attributes and embraces a new way of being and leading—what she calls *Comflluential Leadership.*

Comfluence™ weaves the positive qualities of masculine leadership (analytical thinking, competitiveness, decisive and resilient action) with the feminine side (the ability to connect, build deep relationships both personal and professional, show patience, use reason not ideology to break deadlocks, collaborate and share credit for wins with flexibility and compassion).

Masculine leadership has clear rules and boundaries; it's rigid and hierarchical and easy to adopt. Feminine leadership flows and adapts to circumstances and people's needs; it's more vulnerable and pragmatic and, therefore, can be perceived as passive and even weak. But it is not.

As Linda notes in *No One Stood Up When I Entered the Room,* "The distinction between leading through command and leading through influence is important. When you use your influential leadership, you begin to change the very fabric of your world for the better. You bring people in, they willingly come along on your journey, and you are joined together in the same passion, motivation and vision, which is a powerful formula for sustained success. Like making a patchwork quilt, each piece contributes to make one beautiful, lasting whole."

Our world is changing so rapidly and there are so many challenges confronting us—from global warming to gun violence. Clearly the old way of leading isn't working any longer. We, as leaders, need a new way forward. I believe Linda's Comfluential Leadership model *is* that way.

Peace,
CJ Scarlet
Author of *The Badass Girl's Guide:
Uncommon Strategies to Outwit Predators*

Introduction

PERHAPS YOU ARE wondering where this title comes from, perhaps not at all. Or . . . you know it all too well because you've experienced it.

Early in my life, it was the norm for men to stand up when a woman entered the room, approached a table, or left for the ladies' room. It was also the norm to open doors and assist a woman with putting on her coat. We, as women in the women's movement, basically asked men to stop doing any of this. We wanted equality and thought these "norms" were doing a disservice to the cause. So, this is one reason why no one stood up (anymore). However, there is an entirely different reason that was important to me.

Leadership has been a "private men's club" for hundreds of years. It is a societal structure and expectation that influences every woman who wants to succeed in business, to advance her career, and to lead in a meaningful way. This is a masculine model of leadership characterized by 'command' rather than 'influence.'

It is important for women (and for men) to know and understand this rarified world, and the implications it has on society. We all need to recognize that the imbalance in this model prevents each of us from truly becoming the effective, powerful leader we're meant to be.

My career began in the military, the origin and bastion of the masculine leadership model. I had to learn the command model quickly in order to succeed. Even in the Women's Army Corps (WAC) the model was the same. I became an officer, with all the expectations that my troops would follow my command without question—and stand

and salute when I entered the room or passed them on the base. Thus, the title of this book.

Our leadership mentors and role models have been male for the most part. Whatever background you come from—military, corporate, nonprofit, government, or even your family—the individuals in charge and leading have generally been men, correct? Even if you had a female mentor, her mentor more likely than not was male.

Does this mean that our only choice is to follow this model, to pull from male-only characteristics in order to become a leader?

Absolutely not! So, the question becomes: *how do we engage the feminine aspects of leadership in such a way that we still remain strong and powerful leaders?*

History: Women in Command

When you look back in history, we were and are a very warlike people, sometimes with women in command. If you as the queen needed your subjects to respond to a call to war, you did it with your 'command voice.' You told your people what to do. You commanded your dukes and lords to draft several hundred of their people and bring them, armed, to a specific location. Not surprisingly, they did it with a grumble or two—but they did it.

We women are not the stronger of the two sexes, yet we have fought and fought well. Tales of the ancient gods show the female gods could be just as ruthless as male gods, maybe even more so—for example, the Egyptian goddess Sekhmet or the Hindu goddess Kali, or the Greek goddess Athena. (Pallas Athena was the beloved symbol for the WAC).

Across centuries and cultures, women warriors have stood out in leadership and bravery. Fu Hao (thirteenth century BC) was a Chinese general who led thirteen thousand people in battle, defeating the Shang. Zenobia (third century AD) was the queen of Syria who rebelled successfully against the Romans and became the gold standard for 'strong women' for centuries thereafter. Khawlah bint al-Azwar (seventh century) was a black knight who led an army of women for Muhammad. Mai Bhago (seventeenth century) was a Sikh warrior saint, the only survivor of the bloody battle of Khidrana. In 1778, Molly Pitcher (Ludwig) kept bringing water to the colonial revolutionaries, then took up arms herself and fought courageously. Just to name a few . . . [1]

It is also said that the female is the more deadly of the species. Think the women assassins in World War II using hatpins or poison as a weapon. Or ex-school teacher Nieves Fernandez, a Filipina guerrilla leader who killed two hundred Japanese with homemade guns and survived a large bounty on her head.

It would appear women don't need to be taught command. If we look hard enough, we find thousands more women who have taken command and taken action to change the course of history for their people. They are honored (if they are recognized at all) for their masculine leadership model—command, action, willingness to engage in conflict, aggression, and often, brutality. In almost every case, these women had to disguise themselves as men or take on the leadership role without permission in order to fulfill their purpose and destiny.

Modern Day: The Masculine Leadership Model

Fast-forward to modern American society. Studies show that both men and women exhibit leadership effectiveness, yet the stereotypes persist that leaders are male and that the acceptable characteristics of leadership fit the masculine model.[2] These perceptions come from the powerful role of history where men have held most of the leadership positions in society, and the social model is patriarchal. In my trainings and talks (primarily to female audiences), I often begin this way: "Close your eyes and tell me what you picture when I say the word 'leader.' What comes to your mind?" Almost to a person, among several hundred people I've asked, they describe a man in a suit or possibly some type of uniform.

Men are often confused when women use a strong command style, as it doesn't fit the image that modern society has taught them, and many feel it is just wrong. Statistics as recent as 2019 reveal a gap between a woman's qualifications and her ability to be promoted by men.[3] I know many women (myself included) who have lost their jobs because of this one-sided perception of what leadership is supposed to look like. We're seen as too bossy, aggressive, overstepping our bounds, too competitive—you may be able to fill in more blanks here. If we use only the feminine model, characterized as 'influence' more than 'command,' men tend to perceive us as weak, emotional, unreliable, and ineffective.

An important point to be made here is that women share these same stereotypes of women in leadership! We have been brought up in the same society as men have, with the same history and the same daily messaging about who is the acceptable leader. This is why I have written this book—to break through these stale and absolutely wrong perceptions of what leadership should look like.

I believe it is crucial for society to change this paradigm that limits how effective women and men can be as leaders. We need to create a new model of leadership, which I have named "Comfluence™"—the marriage of command and influence.

Masculine and Feminine Leadership Styles

The difference between male and female leadership styles is a topic that has been studied extensively over the last several years. Yet it hasn't become a topic of conversation around the kitchen or boardroom table enough, from what I hear about women's experiences at work. According to Forbes Coaches Council, women are still lagging behind when it comes to leadership roles in business. Women "are faced with a range of challenges that many of their male CEO counterparts don't have an understanding of . . . preventing many women from achieving their goal of becoming a leader at their company." [4] In 2018, a little over five percent of CEO roles at Fortune 1000 companies were held by women, and with only 11.5 percent of "stepping-stone" executive jobs held by women, the CEO pool is "hardly a plentiful pool from which to boost the number of women at the top."[5]

This is the status of the "private club" of men's leadership.

And how is male leadership succeeding in creating a civilized world that works for everyone? I submit, not very well—perhaps for a few, but not many. We have lived a very long time with the driven, aggressive, unapproachable, overbearing, greedy, rigid, arrogant, entitled leaders in our world who work in a tightly wound power circle (the Good Old Boys Network). Our world has suffered for this with wars, drugs, violence, and too many senseless deaths. This is from leadership power that has leaned too far towards the masculine end of the spectrum and not far enough towards the feminine.

A balance is needed that represents the strengths and positive characteristics of both. If we truly want to make a change in this world before it is destroyed completely, then we must embrace a significant change in how we lead. It will take nothing less than a transformational shift in perspective on what effective leadership truly is.

The Command Voice

As a woman who has spent most of her professional life in the "man's world" of military and corporate leadership, I have a unique perspective on the masculine characteristics of leadership, which can be expressed conveniently in one word: **Command**.

I come by my command voice honestly. From the moment I stepped on base to start my WAC Officer Basic Training to the day I retired as a Major many years later, I was trained to be an expert in command. According to the Army Board Study Guide, "A correctly delivered command will be understood by everyone in the unit. Correct commands have a tone, cadence, and snap that demand willing, correct, and immediate response."[6] You should be standing at attention (in other words—stand up straight; open the throat, mouth, and nose to give amplification, resonance, and projection to the voice). I learned how to pitch my voice 'just so' in order to get maximum volume and attention. When you command someone or a group of some ones, you are not *asking* them to perform a task. No, you are *telling* them with no room for questions or hesitation.

And I was *really* good at it.

When I left the military for the corporate world as a vice president in banking, I continued to use the command voice to 'get the job done' because that was how you led, at least in my experience. Of course, it was about more than just the forceful voice. I was not schooled in being collaborative, vulnerable, or seeking consensus. I expected attention and action.

Working with "civilians" (both men and women) who knew nothing of standing at attention (especially for a woman), it wasn't long before I noticed something was amiss. People did not stand when I entered the boardroom. My commanding voice did not "demand willing, correct, and immediate response." All my relationships stayed formal, and my team and I were never close.

When I left corporate and started my own business, my 'command' leadership style had an even worse effect. Team members who were contract-based and independent did not respond happily to a woman assertively telling them what to do. Turnover was high, as were the costs to my business, not to mention my self-esteem.

Happily, this is not the case today. I know now that the expertise I learned was truly the masculine model of leadership with command at its core. And that is what this book is about.

The Feminine Side of Leadership: Influence

It is the feminine side of leadership—influence versus command—that needs to be recognized and brought out of hiding. If we are going to change the number of women in top leadership roles, then we need to change the model. In this book, I intend to shed light on what leadership has been, what it has become, and what it needs to be for women (and men) to have true influence and for meaningful change to happen.

We'll explore another way—Comfluential Leadership—taking the good qualities of masculine leadership such as analytic thinking, competitiveness, decisive and resilient action, and weave them into the feminine side such as the ability to connect, build deep relationships both personal and professional, exhibit patience, use reason instead of ideology to break deadlocks, collaborate and share credit, and (dare I say it?) show compassion.

My desire for you is to have many aha! moments throughout this book, as you begin to recognize yourself among the stories and lessons I share. I want for you to be able to say that it was written *for you*, that you can see yourself in my journey. And to say that you now know what to do, think, and feel to move towards true, empowered Comfluential Leadership.

Congratulations for doing what you're doing right now! The mere fact that you're reading this shows the leader in you. If that scares you, you are not alone. But I'm willing to bet that you've taken a leadership role at some point in your life—either on purpose, by accident, or by force—and that you would do it again. My hope is that this book will help you do it extraordinarily!

CHAPTER 1

This Is Me

I GREW UP AN only child, with older adults to teach me the social nuances of childhood into adulthood. Added to all those messages from society that I'm sure you can name—the ones about what girls should and shouldn't do—were others laid on my heart by my mother and grandmother, loud and clear. Three things that I could never do:

1. I could not stand up in front of groups of people and speak because I wasn't good at it.

2. I could not make friends on my own without the help of my grandmother.

3. If I did manage to have friends, I could never trust them, so I was to build my protection walls thick and tall because surely these so-called friends would stab me in the back.

No wonder I felt socially inept around kids my age, had few close girlfriends, and stood in the shadows of leadership for so many years!

What I was very good at were all those tasks that are known to lean towards the masculine side—doing, doing, and doing. I could organize almost anything. I was very detail-oriented, with a passion for successful results. I had drive, determination, and a competitive spirit which led me to shine as a swimmer.

I also had the gift of an independent-minded mom who believed in strong women. As high school graduation drew near, I considered becoming a nurse. My mom responded with a categorical "No! Be a doctor. You'll have more power to get things done." Her expectation that I would take a nontraditional role for women is something for which I'm very grateful today.

So, I started my college experience in pre-med, which lasted about a semester. I hated it. I shifted my majors to economics and sociology, and worked in the psychology department and the data center to keep myself busy. As the end of my junior year was looming, it was time to decide what I was going to do.

My dad had served with the Marines before World War II and as a Naval Petty Officer during the war. My parents' recollections of being in a military family, which were an integral part of my childhood, sparked my interest. There were summer programs for both the Navy and the Army. Dad helped me choose which would serve me best—and the Army won. I did the four-week Junior Officer program, and loved it. There was structure I could understand; there were opportunities to manage departments.

With that summer of training, I was accepted in the Student Officer Program, got paid as a Corporal, and had the privilege of being active duty military. I was commissioned a 2LT after graduation, and started WAC's Officer Basic Course at Fort McClellan, AL.

My First Taste of Command in Action

Fort McClellan, AL, was the home of the WAC, which was the women's branch of the (men's) U.S. Army at the time. This post was very unusual for a military base as it was the only base in the world with mirror systems for men and women. Two headquarters, two flagpoles, two commanders each running a corps—one a man, and one a woman.

Here was where I would spend the next four and a half months in WAC Officer Basic Training and later, two years as a Platoon Officer in a basic training company. Even though the number of WACs in the Army was relatively small, we were able to establish a very distinct corps, with our own basic training, our own leadership hierarchy, and our own rules to follow.

As a young woman of twenty-one, my experience with the WACs provided a huge lesson to me which has underpinned my life ever since. Just because women were perceived as the weak minority did not mean we had to embody that. The career female officers could easily have let the male side of the military dictate how the corps was run. Instead, they set their own standards which were, in fact, higher than those of the men. In the seventies, when the women's corps began to be more fully incorporated into the U.S. Army, the WACs actually *lowered* their recruiting standards.

This fact spoke volumes to me, and still does as I recall the remarkable women who trained me and with whom I was privileged to serve. So many of the leaders inspired me: they knew how to use their influential voices to make things happen in a man's world; they knew how to advance their agendas; they were wise and picked their battles, and were incredibly strong.

Being a Woman in the Man's Army

Remember that my strong mother counseled me about choosing a direction that would wield more power and control. And here I was in the military. So, one might think I was positioned to be a fearless leader right from the start. I sound like I was confident in my choice of the military as the natural place to experience being a leader. After all, I had studied the great generals in World War II and thought I understood what it took.

Well, it wasn't that easy. To be honest, I was very afraid that I would not be good enough to be a military leader, especially when it came to leading men. It was indeed a 'man's army' and we were reminded of this the moment we put on our uniforms. For example, we were not allowed to marry or have children, and we had to hold ourselves to a higher standard than men to be accepted for the same responsibilities.

We were expected to be more put-together. We were to follow the physical training manual designed for women, entitled *You Must Be*

Fit,[7] which was intended to bring women to top physical standards; it also concluded with *The Army Way to Health and Added Attractiveness* with advice on skin care, makeup, and hairstyles. While men only had to 'break starch' on their fatigues, we women had to iron every wrinkle out of our uniforms. Everywhere I went an iron followed me!

And then there was the sergeant who actually told me he would walk around the block to avoid saluting a woman officer. Later I would discover that he had been hiding key requests for information so that the unit and I would be written up for dereliction of duty. First I got the unit current on all requests and then I transferred him to Fort Wainwright, Alaska, one of the coldest bases on the planet, to reflect on the error of his ways . . .

What's Merit Got to Do with It?

Call me crazy, but I believed that if I worked hard, honestly, and with integrity, the system would reward me. This was what I had learned from my parents, and what I had done through school, excelling academically and in competitive swimming in particular. Entering adulthood, I thought it would be no different. I had faith that whatever I earned would be the result of merit. Well, I was in for a sobering reality check!

The year was 1973 and I was recommended along with twenty other top-rated Lieutenants for the job of Protocol Officer with the Commander (a four-star General) of the Training and Doctrine command at Ft Monroe VA. We were chosen among the best and the brightest of the Lieutenants stationed at Ft McClellan AL. It then came down to the top two—another woman and me. I went into the final interview secure in my ability and believing I was sure to be selected due to my merit. I felt confident as I stood at attention before the Chief of the General Staff, the man who would make the final choice.

And so it happened. I was the one selected to take this prestigious position! You can imagine how I felt—proud, excited about the recognition, eager to jump into this new experience and do my very best. Yet my mind still asked me, did they really choose the best?

Shouldn't it have been the other Lieutenant? There was a lot of pressure to be perfect or there would not be another WAC in a position of this stature. My predecessors had been reassigned as one got pregnant at a time when that meant instant discharge, and the second had the audacity to put the only umbrella she had over her head and not the foreign dignitary's head when a sudden rain shower began. Needless to say, he was soaking wet when they finally got to their briefing. He was not happy. When asked by her boss why she broke protocol, she noted that a new hat would cost her $200; instead her mistake cost her job and career. I was told that I was the WAC's last hope for having a woman in this position. I had to be perfect for my own career and for the Corps.

Had the Chief of the General Staff not been throwing back a fair amount of drinks at a party a few months later, I never would have found out the truth. He loosened up enough to decide to tell me the real reason why he had selected me for the job. Why was I chosen over twenty capable applicants? Was it my education, my military bearing, my sense of humor, my answers to the interview questions? No, the key differentiator was (Are you ready for this?) *my legs.*

"That was what did it for me!" he said, quite matter-of-factly. I was blown away!! Was my worth based solely on the definition of my calf muscles? And, of course, the next question that immediately crossed my mind was: if I were male, would that criteria ever have been considered?

You can imagine what this did to me. I was now faced with a choice that would have a huge impact on my future: I could fold up like a wilted flower, go through my days as if I didn't deserve this position, and never summon up the confidence around my boss and coworkers to be all I could be. Or . . . I could decide that I was not going to be a disappointment to myself, to the job, or to my corps. Yes, I regretted that it was my legs that got me the job. But I wasn't going to be less of me because of it, so I set out to be the best damn Protocol Officer they had ever seen!

You know the Kelly Clarkson song "What Doesn't Kill You Makes You Stronger?" That was me and the path I chose, and I have never regretted *that* decision.

Standing Out or Standing Down: The Risk of Taking Risks

Taking risks in the military is not always something that is valued. In fact, following the status quo is the norm. As the newest team member of five Protocol Officers for the Training and Development Command General, I followed the lead of the senior members of the team regarding the traditions already established.

One of these was that the Commanding General always selected a chef salad for his entree at lunch, and the Deputy Commander never wanted chef salad in his options. I asked why this was the case, and was told that it was the cheapest item offered to the Commanding General. The deputy, because he ate many of those lunches, was sick and tired of chef salad. I thought this was ridiculous. Surely, there must be something else we could offer.

As a lowly Lieutenant, I hesitantly took it upon myself to have a conversation with the chef to see what we could do. I was surprised that the chef was interested in doing something different too. He was tired of making chef salad in massive quantities each day. Together we created a variety of menus that were unique, interesting, and delicious. The plus was that they cost less than chef salad!

So, step one had been taken. Now I had to take the risk of presenting my idea to my boss, a Colonel, which was terrifying. What if he didn't like it? What if he wasn't willing to try? What if the General fired me? (Yes, that can happen; it is known as being transferred.)

Because my Colonel was a bit timid and compliant, I suggested a wager. Let me present one of my options on the next visit proposal. If the General didn't select it, I would pay the Colonel $100; if he did, we would put the other options into the plans for future visitors to the headquarters. He agreed, rather than get into a discussion with me. The proposed visit went up to the General and back down to us. The lunch options chosen . . . were mine. I was thrilled and got the respect of my colleagues as they had not thought of it.

The lesson: ***Where are you missing opportunities or not taking risks because you have rules that create a blindness to all that is possible?*** Perhaps it is time to take a risk that might be scary and uncomfortable.

Perhaps it is time to question the rules and the status quo, one chef-salad-sized victory at a time.

My assignments in the military included managing a team of men who kept track of all the troops in the six New England states; being selected as a member of the Army Recruitment team to speak at local high schools to recruit graduating seniors into the service; serving as MIA/POW liaison throughout New England; being the Executive Officer for a basic training company (the only officer besides the Company Commander leading two-week and six-week basic training units of one hundred and twenty women); and, of course, becoming a Protocol Officer to a four-star General. Each of these assignments gave me valuable experience I would need and use in my civilian life in corporate as well as in my own businesses.

However, being in the military was not easy, and I did sometimes question my decision about joining. Yet I persevered and made mistakes and, in the end, really began the process of honing the skills of leadership. Little did I know that I would soon be confronted, as so many of us are in adulthood, with my own personal brand of discrimination and judgment—that which comes from our childhood stories and the influences which hold us back from fully stepping into our best selves.

My Journey to Define Leadership

I came out of the military with that command voice I told you about, schooled in command, not in being collaborative, compassionate, or seeking consensus.

Whether drawn from my experience in the Army, modeling my grandmother or mother (as I've mentioned, both of whom were very strong women), or emulating my beloved father's strengths, I had created a very specific perception of how to be recognized as a powerful leader. I had the belief that I always had to be strong, to be imposing, to act confident perhaps even to the point of being arrogant, to embody the masculine qualities of decisiveness, resilience, and assertiveness. I could NOT show vulnerability, only strength. Without this demeanor, how could I possibly lead anyone including myself? This was what I believed.

A significant step towards my awakening to a much more balanced concept of leadership came not from a woman as you might expect, but from a man: my husband.

What happens when a father's strength and a daughter's vulnerability are aligned? When my first daughter was born, and then the second, I watched my husband hold them for the very first time. It was a beautiful picture of love—such awe in his face as he held these tiny creatures in his arms. I saw the power of a child to touch his heart, to bring out the vulnerability in him. And that it was okay to be vulnerable—he could still be strong!

As the girls grew up, my husband's strength held the space for them and allowed them to make mistakes, to experience their emotions and to grow their wings as they flew. His strength was quiet, even soft, but no less reassuring or powerful. This was amazing for me to experience, and he still holds that place for them to this day. And of course, in my heart.

The Yin and Yang of Leadership: Seeds of Comfluence™

My husband's comfort with what I now know are feminine characteristics (which both men and women have within us, of course) inspired me to begin to look at the perception I had created of how to be a leader. To be the best I could be, it was time to look at this aspect of myself. It was time for reassessment and exploration.

Over the next years as I studied successful leaders for my programs and the book I was writing, The Art of Herding Cats: Leading Teams of Leaders, I made some wonderful discoveries about the 'yin and yang' of leadership. I realized that the great women leaders embraced feminine qualities, integrated them with selective masculine qualities, and tapped into their own vulnerability to relate to the people who followed them. They used patience, expressiveness, intuition, flexibility, and empathy to their distinct advantage. They were willing to share their stories of success and failure to show that they were very human and should not be put on a pedestal to be worshipped. They had their struggles and learned in the crucible of experience how best to lead their teams to reach their visions.

I was reminded of Pallas Athena, the symbol of the WACs, of which I had been so proud. She was a goddess who represented not only war but the more 'feminine' side of success like the arts, the professions, wisdom, and guardianship of the household.

As I learned this new definition of successful leadership for myself, I also started to explore where my rigid perspective had come from. Old childhood stories came up and began to make sense to me—the harsh and judgmental words my grandmother often tossed my way that made me feel like I was imperfect, a disappointment, and made me reluctant to step forward confidently. I recalled my mother's cautionary admonition to "build high, strong walls" around me to protect me from trusting others who might stab me in the back. Both my parents sent messages of excelling and stepping into positions that brought power.

These conflicting messages that I had internalized for so many years collided with what I was learning from my own experience and sense of myself. On the one hand, I continually attracted opportunities to step into leadership roles that I was meant to take yet, on the other hand, I constantly felt afraid I wouldn't be good enough, that I would be a disappointment or get hurt.

Can you perhaps relate to this in your own life—a conflict or disconnect between something you know you really want to do or be, and the stories and influences that tell you that you can't? I think all of us bring some of those messages we grew up with into our adult lives, in ways that hold us back from fully stepping into our potential.

With these powerful new insights, I have been able to face and release many of the old stories that held me back and that have kept my protective walls high. I have learned to express my feminine qualities and still be a leader, in fact, an even stronger leader. Vulnerability and being open to trust are not signs of weakness; rather, they are part of building deep, beautiful, trustworthy relationships that lead to success in all kinds of ways.

I learned—needless to say am still and always learning—to embrace the mistakes I made and learn from them. I now share them so that others might not have to go through those same challenges. I've made it my life's work to teach the mindset, the courage, the confidence, and the leadership skills a woman needs to be the best she can be, in her own unique way. This is why I have written this book, to share these insights with you.

CHAPTER 2

Leadership:
What It Is and What It Is Not

GREAT LEADERS IN any business or enterprise possess solid social intelligence, a drive for change and, above all, a vision that allows them to set their sights on the things that truly merit attention. The people who can do this are the leaders who make positive and powerful changes.

One of my favorite definitions of leadership comes from World War II General and United States President Dwight D. Eisenhower, who said, *"Leadership is the art of getting someone else to do something that YOU want done because HE [SHE] wants to do it* [emphasis added]." Eisenhower's point is so simple, yet it is fundamental and appropriate for all areas of great accomplishment: leading soldiers into battle, gaining consensus between opposing political parties, or motivating your team to take the necessary actions to move your goals forward.

When you can help others see the goal AND see the paths to take in order to reach that goal, you will be a tremendously successful leader. This and the following points hold true no matter what you are leading, whether it's your country, troops, business, project, or family.

First, a quick note: You'll notice that I'll be using the term "team" throughout this book. It's because 1) my work involves working with teams or leaders of teams in the private and public sector; and 2) I feel it's a good term to describe any group brought together to work towards a common goal and which requires some form of leadership. This could mean a Fortune 100 department, nonprofit board, ad hoc committee, community organizing group, political campaign team, entrepreneurs, vendors and supporters, change movement founders, or family members. As you read, think about how the concepts I share are relevant to whatever endeavor is speaking to your heart.

The following are what I believe to be important characteristics of effective leaders. They take their vision and define a course that sets a clear direction which shapes and changes the future. They are future-oriented, looking for a vision, and are able to hold it for themselves and their followers. They use their influence and enthusiasm to facilitate setting and accomplishing goals.

Leaders are not only willing to risk; they actively take risks. Leaders are not afraid to give due credit to others, nor of taking the heat if something goes wrong. Leaders are lifelong learners continuously working on themselves and growing in every aspect of their lives.

Top Seven Leadership Traits

Leadership takes on many differing components, factors, and shifts in societal perceptions. However, here are the most useful and compelling traits I find that every good leader should have and/or aspire to develop. By the way, these are not necessarily 'masculine' or 'feminine' qualities.

Which ones do you possess, and which could use improvement?

1. Be Passionate.

When you're excited about your work and your mission, it shows! And it rubs off on others. Passion and positive drive get things done and empower others. Of course, your own passion and conviction go a long way to keep you buoyed up when there are successes to celebrate, especially during those times when the ship feels like it's sinking.

Passion is about vision and the energy, excitement, and joy that surround it. People who know me well and those just getting to know me say that I seem to shine when I talk about my vision and movement. It is very obvious to everyone how I feel about it; there is truly a glow around me. When I am not passionate about a project or idea, that also shows in my face, my mannerisms, and my voice. I change from excited, animated, quick-paced speech and hand gestures to more monotone with no hand gestures. Basically, I just stand there and talk—it's boring.

When I am passionate about my vision, I wake up every morning, and it is the first thing I think about. It is also the last thing on my mind and in my heart when I go to bed. The day is then full of moments of brilliance and success in creating the vision in reality. Passion fuels what I do each day—the activities, the thoughts, the writing, the speaking. As a leader what I do is not a J.O.B. but a passion.

It is this passion that draws others to your team and your movement. They get caught up in the excitement of realizing the vision. The individuals who join you in this passion are those who want to make a difference in the world and see that what you are doing will create that change.

2. Be Organized.

Reaching your goals requires organization and knowing exactly the direction of your business or enterprise. Disorganization literally drains your life energy. When you are frazzled, late for a meeting, distracted by your phone, or always rushing around, you encourage the same behavior in others. Being organized inspires trust and sets the standard for your team. How organization is accomplished is in the particular style of the leader.

This is where your masculine side really does shine. It is that side of the brain that resonates with organization. So, what does that mean? It does not necessarily mean having an absolutely clean desk with everything filed away perfectly, with perhaps only the computer and a pen on the desk and maybe not even that. However, that is what it would look like if you were organizationally compulsive. To be honest, that isn't even my style.

Some people organize by building piles. They know what is in each pile and where it is within the pile. I have seen colleagues, when asked for a particular report or document, go straight to a pile, scan it, and pull the item out perfectly. This is organization, just not what everyone might expect. Being organized in your way, whatever that is, reduces the amount of time you spend trying to find things that are 'lost' such as your to-do list, an email about a meeting that starts in fifteen minutes, etc.

However, while chaos may be your style, it actually causes worry and anxiety in the people who work with you, and it can cost you promotions or lateral moves within an organization. To others you look frazzled, stressed, unproductive (or at least less productive), and out of control. This is not the way a leader shows up.

There are so many tools that you can use to be more organized, which I go into thoroughly in my book and workbook, *Awaken the Leader*. I will suggest, however, that a good practice is to make either the first or last thirty minutes of the day a time to set up the day (or next day), what meetings you have, what projects you need to move along, and what calls or emails you need to make. Caution: Being a list-builder and crosser-off of things on a list, I love to make a very long list of what I need to get done each day. However, this does not always serve moving the vision forward. I find that I do all the little, less important items so that the list has lots of cross-throughs. Do I really accomplish the key items? Maybe not!

Sherri Coffelt, Founder and CEO of Results Partner, taught me the Rule of 3.[8] As you probably know, our brains are not designed for multitasking. I know as a woman you might be saying, "Of course we can multitask. I do it every day. It is the only way I can get everything done in a day!" However, what truly keeps you organized and focused is to choose just three key tasks or goals to do each day. This makes organization manageable for you and your team, and supports you staying on track on your vision.

3. Be Responsible.

You must take ownership and responsibility at all times, even as you are delegating work to others. You're the ultimate go-to person; you have their back. You are the holder of the vision, and your followers depend on you to keep on track and moving forward. Your team must know that you'll be there for them when the sailing is smooth as well as when storm winds blow.

As a responsible leader, your role on the team changes. You are no longer "one of the gang." Taking responsibility sets you apart from the team and requires you to take charge of any problems that occur. You can't assume that someone else will handle problem-solving as it is now your job. You are responsible for ensuring that tasks are completed on time and on purpose. If you want your vision to come to fruition, then you also must be results-driven.

Then there's the difference between responsibility and accountability. Aren't they the same? NO! When you delegate a task to a team member, you are sharing the responsibility for getting it done. You, as the leader, still have the accountability because you are answerable for the outcome of the task and the project. You must be able to know the difference; otherwise projects and tasks will languish in the 'incomplete' column as neither of the parties knows what is expected of them. Some leaders believe that once you delegate, you're not accountable if something goes wrong. Not true! The leader holds both responsibility and accountability, the delegate holds only the responsibility to get it done.

In addition, being responsible also means that you know your team. You know its strengths, weaknesses, and growth potential. Mentoring up-and-coming leaders is part of your responsibility. It is behaving responsibly and having a responsible manner that results in achieving significant success.

4. Be Focused.

We've all seen leaders who go off on tangents, get distracted, and ramble on and on in a meeting. Big problem. Stay focused on the mission at hand. This challenge is one reason I named my book and leadership program *The Art of Herding Cats: Leading Teams of Leaders*. It's targeted to entrepreneurs but the concept holds true for any type of leadership. As John C. Maxwell said, *"A leader is one who knows the way, goes the way, and shows the way."* This means holding and keeping the focus for the organization, the vision, the stakeholders, and the team—the big-picture path as well as the specific work at hand.

The *Harvard Business Review* article "Leadership: The Focused Leader,"[9] reports that truly successful leaders need to have three areas of awareness to be successful in making their visions happen. **The first is a focus inward.** Without looking inward, you become aimless, unable to make key decisions or connect with the internal authentic self. To me this is like trying to sail across the Pacific without a rudder; needing to use your weight and sail to set the boat in the right direction—it can be done but is difficult, time-consuming, and very tiring! As the ancient Delphic maxim goes: "Know thyself."

The second focus is on others. Without this focus, you will be clueless. To me this is like walking around with a blindfold on. You find yourself running into walls, posts, and other impediments, without a really clear idea of where you are and how to get to where you want to be. This is why you have a team, especially one that completes you. Knowing its strengths and weaknesses truly makes the work lighter and everyone more satisfied with the outcome.

The third focus is the outside world. Without it, you can be blindsided. This relates to those individuals and companies that are outside your business sphere, your competition, your allies, your target market, and so on. There is so much knowledge to be gained from competitive analysis and understanding the people you are serving, that without it your vision will not be able to happen in the way you want.

So, a clear knowledge of *me*, *us*, and *them* is critical to successful leadership.

5. Communicate Positively.

Outstanding leaders are excellent communicators—why else would people follow them? As you are responsible for holding the vision, you must be able to communicate that vision to inspire and motivate, as well as articulate the steps along the path to achieve the vision. Remember that people need to be heard and need positive affirmation. When you communicate to your people that their individual work matters for the creation of the big picture, you are validating their worth to the team and to the goals, the mission, and the organization. When your people are on board at that level, you all are unstoppable!

Part of being positive in your communications is also avoiding negative words. Blaming people for what has gone wrong is not a way to inspire them to follow you. Here is a great story to illustrate the effect of positive communication by Bob Nicoll in his book *Remember the Ice and Other Paradigm Shifts.*[10] He worked in a small grocery and gas station near a campground. They had a sign above the cash register that said, "Don't forget the ice." Their ice sales were abysmal, while the gas sales were killer. Bob asked his boss if he could make a slight change in the sign for a couple of weeks to see if it made a difference. He changed the sign to read "Remember the Ice"—and sales soared. Simply changing the negative to a positive made all the difference in the world. *Where are you using negative words, and how can you change them to positive?*

Another key aspect of communicating positively is the Comfluential aspect of command versus influence. Move from *telling* to *asking.* For most of us, being TOLD brings up not-so-happy memories of a strict parent or teacher, or military commander or boss. ASKING is being curious, asking questions, inviting a response. Big difference! As a leader, you gain more cooperation, more collaboration, and more inspired followers by being authentically interested in what they have to say.

6. Listen to your people.

Listening is key to knowing what's going on, not just in a business or enterprise, but also in the lives of everyone involved in the endeavor. Listen to what they have to say and provide positive, productive, and supportive feedback (however, remember that you're not there to solve all their problems or take over their responsibilities). Your people will appreciate your consideration, and the relationships will build motivation and cohesion to work towards your goals. Bonus: you stand to build deep, rewarding, lifelong friendships.

Actively listening to people requires that you pay attention. Keep your eyes on the person talking, not out in the distance or on a piece of paper or your smartphone, but truly on their eyes. Look interested in what they are saying. Having a bored expression on your face is not a way to get them to be open with you. Reflect back to them their enthusiasm and excitement, and be honest with your feelings, as people can detect inauthenticity.

Repeating back what you heard is another excellent way of ensuring you heard what they said correctly. It also validates to people that their message was heard and that if action is required, it will be taken. I also take notes. The main reason is that what people have to say to me is important and I don't want to rely on my memory for key details. I let them know why I am taking notes and ask permission. I have never had someone say "no" when I tell them how important what they say to me is to me.

7. Delegate.

Let's face it. You can't do everything. And even (especially) the best leaders don't go it alone. You need a team so that everyone pitches in and does their part to make everything happen. Yet delegating is the one skill that puts fear in the hearts of many leaders, and can be a challenging skill to learn and use. It's important to know how to take the fear out of delegating such that it becomes easy and effortless. And the truth is that you cannot build anything without inviting in the expertise, energy, and execution of others.

These are the reasons why I am going to spend some time on this aspect.

The keys to delegating successfully? First, it's having people on your team who complete you and are not exactly like you. When you begin with this, you are not fighting over who does what. There is a clear path towards what to delegate and what to accomplish. What if I told you that delegating is the cornerstone to keeping your team alive, active, loyal, and increasing profitability? It's true because you are empowering people to realize the vision, to utilize their talents and passion for a common purpose, to take an active part in its success.

From the standpoint of leadership, you want to use the skills, knowledge, and experience of your people to accomplish your goals. Good delegation is also about giving your people ownership of the work they take on. When they own it and take responsibility for its outcome, great things result.

As your team gets larger, it becomes critical to your success and well-being to become proficient in delegating. Here are three aspects of delegation to be aware of, and potential pitfalls to avoid:

Learn to let go so you can grow. Sometimes the areas that you know you should be delegating are the very ones that are within your comfort zone. You know them well; they are easy for you to do; and at the end of the day, they often bring you joy and fulfillment. However, without delegating you will never have the room to grow into new areas of leadership yourself, much less grow the team leaders you need for your endeavor to thrive. Do delegate the tasks that someone else has the expertise or desire to handle. And do delegate some of the work that keeps you comfortable, but doesn't allow you to grow.

Training is not a waste of time. Busy leaders often feel that they don't have the time to teach others what they know, and believe that it's faster and more efficient to do it themselves. So, they end up not delegating at all—a sure path to burnout as well as unhappy, underutilized teams. Consider starting with those types of tasks which are easy to delegate: tasks that are repetitive, tasks that are research-based in nature, tasks that will teach others something, or tasks that create a plan of action. Surprisingly, as I began to delegate tasks, I found that the people to whom I taught a task (which I had thought would take so much precious time to do) were often better at it than I was. In fact, I often learned something new from delegating instead of holding onto the status quo. Imagine that!

Give authority AND ask for accountability. To delegate effectively, you need to know and trust your people. You will be giving them the responsibility for completing the task and also enough accountability to keep them from coming to you for every little decision. As I mentioned earlier, you don't want to give up both the responsibility and accountability for completion.

Understand that not everyone is strong in all the skills needed to successfully achieve your goals. Many trainers suggest that you use your strengths to improve your weaknesses. I say go with your strengths, and leverage your weaker areas with people who are good in them.

Self-made billionaire founder of Spanx, Sara Blakely, hired a CEO to run the business when Spanx was just two years old. Many (particularly male) eyebrows were raised by her actions because, you know, everyone wants to be the CEO, the head honcho, of their own business! But Sara said it allowed her to focus on the things she was particularly good at as well as helping keep balance in her work-family life. "As soon as you can afford to, hire your weaknesses," she said. "Hiring a CEO was very critical for me to stay on my strengths."[11]

Make delegation work in your favor. For example, if you are not good at the people aspect but are great with numbers, then partner up with a people person to make calls and do presentations. Thus, developing the team and its members' individual abilities can make your team really sing. Look for the golden nuggets in your team, those who want to learn new skills that you can support, or who want to become leaders whom you can train to develop into leaders in their own right.

CHAPTER 3

Are Leaders Born or
Are They Made?

THERE ARE THOSE who believe that leaders are born and not made—the nature versus nurture debate. Leadership in tribes and throughout the animal kingdom is often determined through a fight for control, usually to the death or disabling of the loser. This concept relies on brute strength, and the leadership position is held only as long as the individual is strong. The tribe follows because the leader is supposed to provide protection, not because he or she accomplished anything other than being the strongest member. This type of leader is the "top dog," and not necessarily concerned with building relationships with members of the tribe or being a good motivator; rather, the goal is maintaining tight control over their subjects.

Thankfully, human society and social evolution have come a long way from this model, where much more than brute strength comprises the definition of leadership!

There is talent and skill to leadership. What's the difference? Well, there are several ways to think of it. In general, talent is something you are born with. You have a talent for things that come naturally to you. Skill, on the other hand, tends to be something you learn. However, I feel there is more to it than that. Talent may be what you're born with, but skill is what you do with it. Everyone learns to talk—some become orators. People have to learn to drive—not all of them become NASCAR racers.

Nature vs. Nurture: Maybe It Takes Both?

My mom had tremendous musical talent and performed classical music with her sister on dual pianos. She and her sister spent hours learning and honing the skills and nuances of playing professionally. However, my mother really wanted to learn other types of music, like jazz. Because of her stellar ability with classical music, neither her piano teachers nor her parents would allow any deviation.

So, she wanted me to learn all the things denied to her: dance, ice-skating, and baton. She threw me, as a young child, into everything (except music) regardless of any talent I might have shown. I was shuffled off to ballet classes until I was told I would eventually tower over my dance partners on pointe. (It was *de rigueur* to be shorter in stature.) From there, we went to ice-skating, with the same lack of success. I did not have a natural talent for either, and really wasn't interested enough to try to become good at them.

Eventually, I got to swimming. At last, something I had a talent for! For me, there was nothing like that powerful feeling of cutting through the water with perfect arm strokes, of kicking mightily, and streaking down the swim lane. I had a gift for stroke swimming. Not only could I do it, but I could also teach it. I loved being in the water all day and into the night, so it wasn't long before my talent was melding with my skill building.

The summer before my twelfth birthday I was in heaven. I knew the strokes; I was teaching basic classes; I was performing in synchronized swimming. In fact, my summer swim coach was at a loss as to what to do with me next. The only class I hadn't taken was senior lifesaving. I was way too young and way too small (despite my height) to get the designation. Because you had to be significantly closer to sixteen than I was to take the class and get certified, I wouldn't be able to call myself a lifeguard afterwards, but my coach allowed me to take the class anyway.

To be honest, he never expected me to finish because of my size and age. The guys in the class (and it was all guys) were lean, muscular, tall, and almost double my weight. Of course, we would practice rescue on each other, and I would have to get them out of the pool by myself. Despite all that, the guys always surprised me with encouragement and praise when I was able to perform the skills and as I grew in competence. I was completely committed to excelling at this thing I truly loved.

When it came to the final exam, I had to rescue my coach from drowning, and let me tell you, all of that adult muscle makes one heck of a dead weight. I got him to the side of the pool, and draped his arms over the side. As I was getting out of the pool to haul him up, he began to slip off the side—the rat! I was so exhausted; I knew I didn't have the strength to go down and get him again. So, I made do. I latched onto his shoulder with my nails and pulled. And I got him up, out of the pool, and on the deck.

The guys were shocked—aghast even: I had dug deep into the coach's shoulder and he was bleeding profusely. Everyone stood still, holding their breath, waiting for a yell from the coach. He sat up, looked at his battle wounds, and laughed! He slapped me on the back, and told me I'd done what it took to be a great lifeguard.

Because I had a talent for swimming and learned the skills necessary, I was tremendously successful. I was determined in my intention to achieve the desired result.

Oh, and I did get my lifeguard designation when I turned sixteen.

Leadership Trifecta: Talent + Interest + Skill Development

There is a talent for leadership, that certain something which urges someone to take on leadership roles and want to learn everything it will take to excel. There are people who don't have the talent and don't question it. Just like ballet for me. I didn't have the talent so I wasn't interested in doing everything it would take to become a ballerina.

However, if you *are* questioning your leadership ability, then you probably have the talent and "urge." What you need is to develop the skills and qualities. What I find to be the beautiful outcome of the pursuit to become an exceptional leader is that these qualities and skills will help to make you a more exceptional WOMAN! Read on and answer the following questions for yourself:

Energy/Endurance. Energy and endurance do not require perfect health; they require that you take care of yourself as needed. That is a skill people must learn for and about themselves.
Do you have the physical ability to go, do, and be all the places, tasks, and personas required for leadership?

Humility. No one is born humble. A newborn baby is the most selfish, tyrannical being on the planet! Some personalities may be more prone to humility, but it is something we learn from our family, society, and experiences in being a human interacting in society.
Dictators believe they are better than everyone else; leaders appreciate that they are just as human as everyone else.
Do you believe that you can develop the ability to lead humbly?

Excellent Communication Skills. Communication has a talent component, based on a personality (such as charisma) that you're born with. However, you can learn to communicate more effectively in a leadership role. And if you are passionate about your message, your talent for communicating it will blossom! People need to know about your passion in order to follow you—your vision, strategy, direction, and commitment are important to communicating clearly.
Can you speak and write about these things in a compelling manner?

Daring. I agree that some people are just naturally more daring than others. However, many daring people are that way because they've been through experiences where they had no choice but to risk everything, or they didn't have anything to lose, so why not take the leap? But daring also includes making decisions, a key component of leadership. You learn good decision-making through information, learning—and practice. You will make mistakes; we all do. Someone once said, "Good decisions come from experience, and experience comes from bad decisions."

Where do you take risks or make good decisions that last?

Integrity. This is the practice of being honest, showing consistent ethical and moral values, and being reliable in your actions. It's thought of as honesty and truthfulness. I believe we are faced with ways to practice integrity all our lives—perhaps a lifelong thing to learn and develop.

Do you do as you say? Do you walk your talk?

Talent encourages and might underpin these traits, but all of these are skills that can be learned, developed, and practiced. And wouldn't you say these are important characteristics to possess in order to excel at anything in your life?

CHAPTER 4

Leadership and Management:
Not the Same Thing

SOME DEFINE LEADERSHIP as getting work done through others. To me, this is more management than leadership. In today's world, leadership is more about investing in people and trusting that they have the skills to do the work, and collaborating with others to accomplish the goals. True leadership has little to do with hierarchy or supreme authority.

The manager's job is to plan, organize, and coordinate. The leader's job is to inspire and motivate. In his seminal book, *On Becoming a Leader*, Warren Bennis, a pioneer in leadership studies, lists many of the differences between leaders and managers:[12]

- *The manager administers; the leader innovates.*

- *The manager is a copy; the leader is an original.*

- *The manager maintains; the leader develops.*

- *The manager focuses on systems and structure; the leader focuses on people.*

- *The manager relies on control; the leader inspires trust.*

- *The manager has a short-range view; the leader has a long-range perspective.*

- *The manager asks how and when; the leader asks what and why.*

- *The manager always has their eye on the bottom line; the leader's eye is on the horizon.*

- *The manager imitates; the leader originates.*

- *The manager accepts the status quo; the leader challenges it.*

- *The manager is the classic good soldier; the leader—well–not so much.*

- *The manager does things right; the leader Does the Right Thing.*

What Makes Management Different from Leadership?

Most dictionaries have very similar definitions for both "management" and "leadership:" *get a group to a goal.* How you select the goal, and then how the group gets to the goal, however, are key to the difference in the roles.

For a manager, the goal comes from someone else. The manager's job is to allocate people and resources to complete the tasks necessary.

For a leader, the goal is something a person has envisioned, and leaders inspire people to come along for the ride.

The following excellent description of the difference between managers and leaders is taken from ChangingMinds.org.[13]

Managers are subordinates who have subordinates. So, while they may be in charge of some people or things, they are not the top of the food chain. Thus, your manager has to worry about their boss as much as you worry about yours. Dealing with subordinates is very transactional. "Do the task I assign you and you will continue to receive your salary." Effective, but not very inspirational.

Managers tend to come from comfortable and 'normal backgrounds,' and tend to prefer stability. This can lead to risk aversion.

On the other hand, *leaders have followers.* Because following is completely voluntary, the benefits are more transformational than transactional. Instead of the "do A to get B" style of managers, leaders charismatically attract people to their cause with intangible or personal benefits, such as becoming a better person or rescuing an endangered species.

Because leaders are pursuing THEIR OWN vision, stumbling blocks and misdirection are expected—even enjoyed. Where a manager likes things nice and safe, a leader seeks and finds the potential that only risk can provide.

There is a reason people confuse management and leadership. A manager has a position of power while a leader is powerful. The two are not the same. Managers tend to have a grounded mentality and use that to navigate the work. Managers are more present-focused, while setting and achieving the objectives of the organization. Managers prefer to control their environment and can be very results-oriented. They use their more positional authority to make work happen. Risk is not something managers like to take. They may take the credit for the results accomplished and shift the blame to others. Managers can also be lifelong learners; however, their learning focus may be more in the line of skills development.

Interacting with Others

Another distinction between leaders and managers is how they interact with people. As a necessity, leaders are good with people. After all, who's going to follow someone who is insulting, conceited, tactless, and/or overly grumpy? Good leaders are equally brilliant at giving praise and taking blame. They are inspirational.

While a good manager can be inspirational, the position does not require it. The primary focus is getting the job done; personality is secondary.

In simpler terms, *people look to their managers to assign them tasks; they look to their leaders to define their purpose.*

As different as leaders and managers are, they both need to nurture skills, develop talents, and inspire results that lead to success.

The late management guru Peter Drucker said: *"The task is to lead people. And the goal is to make productive the specific strengths and knowledge of every individual."*

Where Management and Leadership Overlap

Just because leadership and management are different doesn't mean that they don't overlap. While leaders appeal to the heart and managers to the mind, someone who does both is going to be stronger in their role as leader OR manager. *Leaders frequently manage, and managers have the potential to lead.*

Do you think that Winston Churchill only delivered speeches inspiring the beleaguered British to first enter and then hold fast during World War II? No, he was the Prime Minister of the United Kingdom, a high-ranking manager, but a manager just the same.

As a leader, Dr. Martin Luther King Jr. spoke to hundreds of thousands of people and promoted peaceful protests for civil rights. As a manager, he formed and directed the Southern Christian Leadership Conference (SCLC).

Rarely do people become famous for their managerial skills. However, how many famous leaders do you know of who had nothing to do with the implementation of their vision?

So, the next time you're looking at a manager, ask yourself, "If it were her vision, would she be a leader?" If the vision is clear enough and the passion strong enough, that manager is well on her way to becoming a leader.

When becoming a leader, it is important to know how that differs from becoming a manager. Rear Admiral Grace Murray Hopper once said, "You manage things; you lead people." She was a pioneer of computer programming and an inventor in the forties, when women were rarely welcomed into leadership in the field. She was a Rear Admiral in the U.S. Navy, and the U.S. Navy *Arleigh Burke*-class guided-missile destroyer U.S.S *Hopper* was named for her. I would say she knew what she was talking about.

What a Great Combination Looks Like

There were these two guys who met in college in 1934. In 1938, they rented a garage, scraped together some cash and a drill press, and then went to work on a device to test sound equipment. It caught the attention of the Walt Disney Company. By the end of 1940, these two pals moved out of the garage, gave employees bonuses, and started making donations to charity. In 1942, the company implemented a health plan that insured all of its employees and built its first building with a versatile open-floor plan—that just happened to spark creativity.

Were the two guys managers or leaders? Well, they had a vision and they made it happen, so they obviously had both skills well under control. By the way, those friends were Bill Hewlett and Dave Packard, and their vision is still going strong, over seventy-five years later, even though they have both passed.

Hewlett and Packard also liked the concept of "management by walking around." In their management positions, by regularly visiting where the "real work" happened, they stayed in touch with the team and kept up to date on what was really going on in the company – preserving their roles as leaders.

What Happens When You Have One Without the Other

We know what a great combination of leadership and management looks like. What happens when you have one without the other?

Think of all those great 'big-picture' thinkers. They always have brilliant ideas and absolutely no clue as to how to achieve them. That's leadership without management. Unless they have partners who see the details and have the ability to implement, they're basically unemployed dreamers.

A sport referee best exemplifies the reverse—management without leadership. The goal is for one team to win the game by following the rules. The job of the referee is to ensure the team follows the rules. Referees do not have a unique vision; they are not even allowed to have a goal of their own. They just manage the two teams during play. While employable, you can see how the personal growth of a referee could be limiting.

Are You Leading or Managing?

So, how do you know if you're leading or managing? Find out by answering this series of questions created by the *Harvard Business Review:*[14]

1. ***Are you counting value or creating it?*** Keeping track of every little thing is counting value—a solid trait of managers. Leaving the team to do what it needs to do while you do something else is creating value—a sign of leadership.

2. ***Do you have circles of influence or power?*** This is similar to the concept that leaders have followers and managers have subordinates. The more people you have asking for your advice, especially if they are outside of your team, the more people see you as a leader.

3. ***Do you lead people or manage work?*** If your focus is on the specific task instead of on motivating the person performing the task, you are still in manager mode.

Moving from a mindset of being a manager to that of becoming a leader is essential to successful leadership. You might be afraid that you can't do it, that you don't have the skills to be the leader whom you would want to follow. That is perfectly natural. In fact, I would be concerned if you were NOT afraid. Armed with this information and awareness of the characteristics of leadership, however, you're well ahead of the game!

I understand your feelings well. Remember, in the military I stepped into my management responsibilities with a fair amount of uncertainty and at times, self-doubt. I just did my job the best I could, and never thought I was actually taking on leadership roles. I was what I call a "reluctant leader." Read on . . .

CHAPTER 5

Reluctant Leaders

D O YOU KNOW who makes up a large portion of reluctant leaders? *Women.*

There's a reason for the saying, "Behind every great man is a great woman." I prefer the more modern variant: "Behind every great man is a supportive and devoted woman to keep his head on straight!" In their traditional role of "supportive person," women leaders generally start out supporting someone else.

Eleanor Roosevelt is a perfect example. She accomplished many things—including chairing the United Nations Human Rights Commission—as the First Lady, a job title that had no substance at the time. (Let's not forget, in the thirties and forties there were few positions of power and leadership available to women at all). It was Eleanor's position as First Lady which allowed her the platform to become a pillar of leadership that gave her a permanent place in history.

Then there is the first woman president, Edith Wilson. We have never had a female president; how can this be? It is quite an interesting tale. At the end of World War I, then President Woodrow Wilson had a stroke which made it impossible for him to run the country. Edith stepped in. She had already been screening Wilson from advisors and had access at a high level to documents and information. She would never let Wilson resign and the Vice President take over. She screened all his mail, messages, and visitors and handed back responses that often did not look like the President's handwriting. She called it 'stewardship.' I would call it presidential.

Another aspect of leadership is making change to create a better future than the one currently on the horizon: the change agent. This type of leader exhibits the courage and fortitude to take a stand and speak out. Not a conformist, this leader does not require a formal position—their motivation is the challenge of making change, of seeing something better happen. Anyone can take up the leadership mantle; there are no right skills or formal authority needed to take this dare. Change agents frequently are reluctant leaders, individuals who are "just doing their job," or who are driven by their passion to see change happen.

A Leader—Who, Me?

And then there's me. As a nonconformist who was a bit awkward, nerdy, and quirky, I never really saw myself as a leader, even though I actually was one. As a Major in the United States Army, I brought together very high-powered leaders, including four-Star Generals, to discuss matters of importance. As this was my job, I didn't see it as leadership. Overall, I spent a decade in the military, and forty years in and around the corporate world. And, yes, in leadership roles.

Even with these successes, I was always the one behind the curtain who just made magic happen and who hated to be publicly recognized for it. It was always my team or my client who deserved the kudos. I was very successful at hiding.

It wasn't until many years later that a total stranger in a workshop came up to me to say, "I thought you would lead us in this exercise. It is what I expected of you."

Where did she get that idea? Well, she apparently saw leadership qualities in me that I didn't see in myself, and believed that I was the right person to stand up and lead in this situation. Female, male, reluctant or not, being a strong leader means you do the things that others are not willing or in a position to do.

Reluctant Leaders in Our Midst

A more recent example of a reluctant leader is Malala Yousafzai, who couldn't stay silenced, even as a child, watching girls being denied the basic right to education. She didn't 'choose' to be a leader, but when she was faced with a situation that needed change, she stepped into leadership, even with all its risks. And look at what she has built as a result!

We can also turn to the high school students who witnessed the horrible shooting of seventeen of their peers at Marjory Stoneman Douglas High School in Parkland, FL. One moment they were being teenagers, doing what teenagers do, assuming a safe world and unlimited possibilities in their future. And then . . . everything changed. One group banded together to do something about it, and became advocates for stronger gun laws, speaking for students nationwide who worry that their school will be next. There were undoubtedly leadership qualities that rose to the surface to compel these students to action, but it's safe to say that not one of these young people CHOSE this role without reluctance. Their anti-gun violence movement went global and they were awarded the 2018 International Children's Peace Prize. As reported in the Miami Herald, "March For Our Lives leaders David Hogg, Emma González, Jaclyn Corin and Matt Deitsch received the award during a ceremony in Cape Town, South Africa. Anti-apartheid leader Desmond Tutu, the winner of the 1984 Nobel Peace Prize, presented the group with the award and said he considered the movement to be one of the most significant instances of youth-led activism in recent memory."[15]

Of course, we have heard about these exceptional leaders in the past and in our society today, those who have led global movements and changed history forever. Yes, they are exceptional leaders, and they are exceptional—reluctant—leaders making change in ways large and small.

We women take leadership roles in our personal and professional lives all the time, often without realizing or accepting that therefore *we are leaders*. This is what I began to learn back in WAC Officer Basic Training those many years ago, when I saw what stepping into leadership looked like by watching the female officers running the WAC command so effectively. It took me some years of living and learning to finally accept that, yes, I am a leader, and this is how I want to live my life. And, in fact, I completely changed careers in order to fulfill this vision for myself. This is now my mission in my work: to teach women how to do the same, to become the leaders they are meant to be.

How about You—Are You Indeed a Leader?

Think about how leadership might appear in your own life. Are you organizing volunteers for your children's school? Have you produced successful galas or fundraisers? Do people look to you when something needs to get done? Do you enjoy inspiring and motivating others? These are all aspects of a leader. Here is a fun little quiz for you to take to find out if you are a leader.

Top Ten Secret Indicators of Women Leaders

Please check all the boxes that apply to you:

- ❏ You thoughtfully plan and cook nutritious meals, carefully choosing ingredients and considering the dietary needs of your guests, even if you never receive a "thank you."

- ❏ You're called upon to organize the cookie, clothing, food, Get Out The Vote, etc. drive—organizing everything and making sure it's done right.

- ❏ You plan the chores for the family and coordinate getting them done.

- ❏ You make breakfast, make lunch, and make sure your family has everything necessary for the day before you go to work (at home or outside the home).

- ❏ You are chosen to organize the family reunion, block party, or potluck. You arrange all the travel, accommodations, food, etc., so no one will get lost or go hungry.

❑ You are picked for a committee even before you join the organization.

❑ You motivate everyone to get out of bed and start the day, even when you would like to push the snooze button a few more times.

❑ You step forward and volunteer even when you don't know what it's for.

❑ You expertly direct how to put together the Christmas toys even though the instructions are written in Swedish.

❑ You are the one people look to for answers.

Guess what? If you selected even ONE of the boxes, you ARE a leader!

CHAPTER 6

Change Agents and Movements

A S YOU MIGHT expect, even spending a lot of time in a 'man's world,' I have been around women all my life, whether at home, school, the military, corporate, and now, my practice. Even with our gender heritage designed to keep us silent (more on this in Chapter 8), I have found that women have a fire in the belly about something that needs to be changed. Often it does not appear to be world-changing, but when realized it can have a monumental impact on those who experience it.

Why are movements so important? Why is this where women often show their leadership? How do you find the time to fit this into life? These are the questions I often hear from the women I know and work with.

Let's see how we might answer them.

Why Are Movements so Important?

First of all, let's define "movement." According to Merriam-Webster Dictionary, movement is *a series of organized activities working towards an objective, also: an organized effort to promote or attain an end.*[16] This is a handy definition to start us off. I would add: *the type of movement that changes the world.* And there is much, much more to it.

In an exercise that I do with attendees at my "Reclaiming the Dream" workshop, I find that the women in the class don't even remember having a dream, much less a movement. I remind them that they probably do have a dream—something they have always wanted to do, be it write a book, run a marathon, travel the world, have a successful business that makes six figures, bring the arts back into schools, provide food for the homeless, and so on. There is usually a collective sigh and a nodding of heads: *Oh yeah, I remember that!*

I ask them, "Where is this dream? Did you put it in a beautiful box, wrap a gorgeous ribbon around it, place that big bow on it, and put the box in the closet, way in the back behind the ski equipment you might pull out someday? When was the last time you saw that box? When was the last time you even realized it might be there?"

The room grows very quiet and there is often a wistful look of bewilderment or disappointment. They didn't even realize they had a dream, much less take a leadership role in moving it forward.

These dreams are what can become movements with the power to change people's lives as well as heal the planet.

In the last several years, there has been an increase in the visibility of key movements. The Women's March was a worldwide protest on January 21, 2017. "The goal of the annual marches is to advocate legislation and policies regarding human rights and other issues, including women's rights, immigration reform, health-care reform, reproductive rights, the environment, LGBTQ rights, racial equality, and freedom of religion, workers' rights, and tolerance." According to organizers, they intended to "send a bold message to our new administration on their first day in office and to the world that women's rights are human rights."[17] The march happens once a year. Between the marches, there is silence.

Shootings in schools have had several protests, especially since the shooting I mentioned earlier at Marjory Stoneman Douglas High School in Parkland, FL, which happened on February 14, 2018. In response to this horrific event was the March for Our Lives (MFOL), a student-led demonstration in support of legislation to prevent gun violence in the United States. It took place in Washington, DC., on March 24, 2018, with over eight hundred eighty sibling events throughout the United States and around the world. It was planned by Never Again MSD in collaboration with the nonprofit organization Every Town for Gun Safety. Again, since that time has the power of this demonstration gone underground? Have we been diverted to other challenges in the world with this taking a back seat?

I have been told that this "be boldly visible–pull back into the shadows" describes the millennials' strategy. It appears that they look at the history of the 1960s and 1970s and say that is not for them. They use a march to identify the challenge and to gain supporters to the cause. Then, the issue is moved to social media where it is discussed and championed. Granted, social media is a powerful tool; however, this effort only speaks to a certain wedge (if they see it at all) and has a relatively short attention span. The result? The movement gets legs and begins to move, then the energy for it peters out until the next time there is an anniversary of some tragedy, or a new tragedy.

Sustaining momentum in any change effort is critical to its success.

Let's Talk About the MOVE in Movement . . .

I clearly remember in the 1960s that there were protest marches regularly. Some were peaceful and others not so much. Yet, the movement was out there where the nation could see it. There was no hiding in the shadows or getting diluted in the anonymity of social media and the internet. In the world today, with all the news media and various media feeds going all the time, we are bombarded by information and stories to the point of being overwhelmed. It is very easy for a movement to move out of the spotlight as something else more sensational takes over. As the newspaper industry says, "If it bleeds, it leads!" The same is true for social media—the "shock factor." In fact, it's part of the business model and the algorithms (tech-run not human-run) that decide what we see on social media on a moment-by-moment basis.

So even though there are very important issues that need our attention and changes that need to be made, why aren't they in our face daily? Why do such important issues become so much background noise, and changes never happen?

If you have ever been in a meeting focused on planning a cause, a political rally, or a protest march or demonstration, do you remember how that experience felt to you? You were face-to-face, side by side, bumping elbows or fists, "live" with the group, hearing and seeing and palpably *feeling* the energy of the crowd and the passion. It was electric, wasn't it? THAT's momentum. It's about being out and moving, with all five senses engaged and the power of a group of people together, all moving in one direction, all with a common goal.

A successful movement needs to be multimedia, not just social media. So, how can we bring people together in a real way? Well, ***the essence of a movement is . . . MOVING.***

Visibility accelerates your impact. There are two key reasons for focusing on visibility to move and sustain a movement:

1. *To keep it top of mind*—this is true for not only change-the-world kinds of movements, but also for your business. If you are not top of mind, you become part of the background noise, you do not become known, no one finds you, and nothing gets done. You want to stay in front of people because they get busy; they forget about the message; they might feel lukewarm about the issue but after repeated exposure they get excited; potential funders want to see that you're out in public which indicates you're worthy of support.

2. *Proliferation*—I am always amazed at the number of groups working on the same issue, when I didn't even know it was an issue. When the movement is splintered into smaller local organizations, the power of numbers doesn't get leveraged. The movement stays local and massive change is not realized. We need to learn about others doing what we are doing and get them on board. By the way, these same organizations are all going after the same grants and donation dollars—why not find ways to collaborate and use that money for more impact?

Find the movers. We who are seasoned and experienced can lend that wisdom to those who are the next leaders. "Millennials are geared to create impactful change in the nonprofit sector," says Sheryl Chamberlain of the Forbes Nonprofit Council.[18] As chair of the Hult Prize Foundation which promotes the intersectionality between social change and start-up culture, Sheryl sees in action the ways in which millennials run businesses, nonprofits, and startups, adding innovative thinking and freedom to solving the world's problems.

Let's make intergenerational connections around our common causes and passions for change to be stronger together.

Make the movement your business. Passion and purpose seed an area for change. To become a movement, that seed of an idea needs nurturing in the form of structure, organization, relationship-building and allies, effective communication, and a system to attract support. It sounds like running a business, doesn't it?

If you are germinating that seed of an idea, starting a movement, or managing an ongoing change endeavor, look at it through the lens of a leader running a business; the structures are the same. I have mentioned Dr. Martin Luther King Jr. as a leader and a manager. The SCLC, which he helped found and grow in 1957 (and it is still active today), is a good example to learn about and emulate how Dr. King brought people together, collaborated with other organizations, and spread a clear message of his purpose.

The Need for Change and Change Agents

Change agents are frequently reluctant leaders "just doing their job" (described in Chapter 5) and they just happen to be making a significant difference.

You can't hide from it. *Change is one of the only constants in this world*, although the old concept also included death and taxes. In fact, change is moving at an even faster rate in the digital age.

When I entered college as a freshman (back in the sixties), we were given a dress code book that told us what we could wear to class, to dances, to church. The dorms were locked at curfew hour, and we were not allowed out after 10:00 p.m. on weekdays and midnight on weekends. Men were not allowed in the dorm other than at the front desk. I was a rebel and violated so many of those rules, including working in the data center from 9:00 p.m. to 6:00 a.m., wandering the campus with one of my male coworkers to find a toilet, wearing pants when the temperature was barely above zero, and so on.

After almost one hundred years of existence, the year after I graduated, the college started allowing coed dorms, and suspended clothing restrictions. That sudden!

"Change happens at the speed of trust," as Stephen M.R. Covey so beautifully states. As humans, we have the ability to visualize, adapt, and change. If you want something different, then you have to be different. As women, more often than not we see the need for change in the world before men. It is part of our makeup to be visionary, creative, collaborative, and so on—feminine leadership qualities.

Making Change Often Means Changing Ourselves

As a woman and business owner, I knew that in order to realize my vision of the future, I needed to make significant changes in how I worked. I went from paper-dominant to online and digital, from telephone exclusive to email, and then to texts and private messages on social media. One of the hardest shifts (and one I still have not embraced fully) is social media. I know that it is a powerful way to get the message of the movement out to huge audiences. I also stated very clearly to a business coach with whom I was working that I would never speak on large stages or do radio or television (more on that in a later chapter). Surprise! I have spoken on stages in front of over six hundred, had a radio show for two and a half years, and have been a guest on several television shows. Oh, by the way, I also said I would never write a blog or a book. Interesting that this is my second solo book and I have six collaborations.

With every step I've taken to change, either eagerly or kicking and screaming, the benefits have been worth it in terms of opening new opportunities for growth.

Perhaps there are things that you've said a defiant (or quiet) NO! to which might be blocking your ability to affect change?

Companies and people who don't or can't change become rigid, outdated, anachronistic, and unable to keep up with the times. Looking at the Fortune 500, only twelve percent remain today from the list created in 1955. The rest either went bankrupt, merged with or were acquired by a larger company, or dropped from the top 500 with decreased yearly revenue.

Ann Salerno and Lillie Brock, cofounders of The Change Cycle™ series, note that there are six stages to change:[19]

1. *Loss: Fear, Cautious, Paralyzed*

2. *Doubt: Resentment, Skeptical, Resistant*

3. *Discomfort: Anxious, Confused, Unproductive*

4. *Discovery: Anticipation, Resourceful, Energized*

5. *Understanding: Confidence, Pragmatic, Productive*

6. *Integration: Satisfaction, Focused, Generous*

You and your organization or team could be anywhere in this cycle. The importance is to know where everyone is on the cycle so that they understand and can continue to move towards integration. It is a cycle and therefore will continue to repeat, so assessing regularly and being flexible is necessary.

Something else that is important to understanding change: How do you and others react to change? The following is a four-box model. The two axes are people/task-oriented and fast/slow-paced. It breaks down this way:

1. *Fast-paced/task-oriented = Driver/Dominance—give them the bottom line, then the details.*

2. *Fast-paced/people-oriented = Expressive/Influencer—show them how this is the latest and greatest.*

3. *Slow-paced/people-oriented = Amiable/Steadiness—show them the benefits of the change and how it will affect the people.*

4. *Slow-paced/task-oriented = Analytical/Conscientious—show them all the details and all the numbers.*

Knowing the style of the people with you on this journey gives you guidance on what to say, how much to say, and when to say it. Taking the right action makes changes easier to handle and faster to see happen.

How Do You Feel about Being a Change Agent?

I have said that women see changes that need to happen and because of that they step into a leadership role to make them happen. They are reluctant leaders or changemakers, but leaders all the same. However, I am sure you could be saying right now, "Nope, not me!" Well, since you can't avoid change happening, here are some things to consider:

- Once again, *change is inevitable*; the world is changing faster than we will ever know. And, some of these changes are not for the better. Look at our water, our food, our air, our climate for some clear examples. Without change agents, these will continue to deteriorate and make life more unbearable for us and for future generations.

- *Expect and manage change*, rather than dreading and becoming a victim of it. If you don't step into leadership to take on changing something about which you are passionate, you then become equivalent to the person who complains but sits back and does nothing.

- *Take back your personal power.* Put a stake in the ground for your personal movement. Support it, nourish it, lead it, and allow the world to change for the better. Join others who are working on the same thing or an adjunct cause. There is strength in numbers.

- Lead and *create a better future* than the one on the horizon, as a change agent, as a leader.

- Have the courage and fortitude to *take a stand and speak out* with the power of your convictions. Look to the recent movements and protests. See the power of their convictions.

What's Needed to Start and Nurture Your Movement

Passion, courage, and a vibrant vision. A leader needs to have self-direction and personal motivation in order to develop a movement that will be successful. Being driven to achieve your vision is what every leader strives to become an expert in. Even reluctant leaders want to see the fruits of their labors grow. From my work I know that stepping into your leadership voice takes courage.

Whether you are creating a gala event to raise money for your nonprofit or creating a multimillion-dollar business, you are motivated by that big, bold, compelling, vibrant vision of the future you have designed. This is what drives you to reach the pinnacle of success. It's that passion that gives you the courage to step up and lead.

Set the tone, standards, and milestones. Being conscious of the achievements and the performance of your team, sponsors, donors, and followers is an ongoing responsibility for you as the leader. Your inspiration and drive to make things happen provides the necessary role model. If, as a leader, you don't set the tone and work ethic, then you will not see the standards of achievement that define the success of your movement. It is key to have a clear set of milestones upon which to nurture and monitor the progress to success.

On the front lines with your troops (team). Looking at leaders of critical movements like civil rights, women's rights, and wartime battles, successful leaders are not just sitting in the headquarters taking phone calls and looking at maps. They are out on the front lines.

General Douglas MacArthur stands out for me as one of these exceptional leaders. His command in World War II was very powerful. He was always driven to take on the next mission, and would let nothing stand in his way, literally. He strode purposefully onto the battlefield, guiding his men from up front in the direction the battle would progress. He was confident in and passionate about his vision of the battle *and he never looked back.* He knew that his troops were following him. When he looked to the left, he saw his comrade in arms, General George Patton, leading his men as well. While the leadership style of both men was Command and they had no concept of Influence, they still are role models for drive and for hands-on, courageous leadership.

Momentum, drive, and forging a clear path. Did you know that, typically, your followers will have *about fifty percent of the drive* they see in you? When we are passionate and driven about something, a mistake we often make is assuming that everyone else feels the exact same way we do and that they'll put in the same amount of effort. The hard truth is that this is rarely the case. If you want to see one hundred percent in the results, then they need to see you putting out two hundred percent effort!

I have experienced what it feels like to have your senior partner, your leader, go off the grid because of personal challenges. It is not pretty as the team flounders and loses momentum. As any serious bike rider knows, losing momentum on a hill could mean death or, in this case, in a serious movement or business. I'm sure you have experienced times when your boss or leader lost momentum, commitment, or interest—and things just seemed to fall apart.

This is not to say that life doesn't happen, or that people won't get sick or leave suddenly for personal reasons. Having a contingency plan can keep that energy high and performing. Making those plans and communicating them to everyone will go a long way towards helping you successfully meet those inevitable challenges that can stop a movement or business dead in its tracks.

And what do you do when 'life happens' to you, or your own momentum begins to wane? Or, when the naysayers of the world doubt you and encourage you to quit (sometimes with the best of intentions)? In those moments, remind yourself of what motivates you and your followers. Revisit your "why"—your vision—the change you sought to make that started this whole thing. Remind yourself of the prize: changing the world for the better. With these strategies, you'll soon reignite the energy needed to rebuild the drive to achieve.

"I Don't Have Time to Create a Movement"

If you are a business owner or entrepreneur, you may be saying to yourself, as I did, that you have no time or energy to put towards creating and growing a movement. *I am going to call you on that!!* You have chosen not to follow the path of the corporate world. You have chosen your own path; to create a business that satisfies your soul and will make a change in the world. Look at it this way: in your business, a movement might be increasing your clients from just one to five. In a start-up, that can be a significant shift towards profitability and success.

You also can think about how you can use your business to fund your nonprofit work. The goal of my business is to fund a social entrepreneurial foundation from the profits. This foundation will encourage grant applications from groups that address women's challenges, i.e., abuse, trafficking, child endangerment, school shootings, drugs, removal of the arts from schools, women's health, clean water, hunger, and so much more. It has been found that women will support causes for women and girls over more general populations. *Why shouldn't your movement be one of those on their giving radar?*

How Do You Find the Time to Fit This into Life?

Our lives are extremely busy, especially as women. We have obligations to family, work, faith, social organizations, networking groups, volunteering, and ourselves. Often it appears there is no space on our plate to add anything else—like creating and nurturing a movement. Well, what if your movement were part of your work? What if it became your volunteering, social, and networking experiences? What if you could bundle your activities in such a way that you accomplish more in less time?

Schedule your time. Time management is a topic that has been on the training agenda for ages. We take classes over and over again hoping that this time the concepts will take hold. I don't use my electronic calendars at all consistently. I keep Outlook up only because my appointment scheduler is linked to it. Also, I have seen too many friends and colleagues have the programs crash and lose all their data.

Now, with everything in the cloud, I believe it is better, yet I still distrust. Call it age; I call it caution.

I don't know about you, but I wander through office supply stores looking at planners, trying to see if there is something better than what I have to keep track of my time and activities. Personally, I have used and abused many a style of planner and finally found one that funnels my energy. I go into time management, organization, and planning in much more detail in my book and workbook, *Awaken the Leader.*

Delegate, delegate, delegate! In Chapter 2, I talked about delegation as a key ingredient for leadership success. This is never truer than in a change effort or movement-building! Delegating activities is an effective way to keep the movement moving forward and maintain its momentum. Key thought: As you delegate, regularly stop and look at where your focus is—on that beautiful vision of the change you want to make in the world, or on the mud at your feet? Leadership requires that balance. So, when you're in the mud in the trenches, pull yourself up and out, dust yourself off, and begin again to focus upward. Remind yourself why you're doing this and how many will benefit from the change you are creating.

Generate your own inspiration. On the movement journey, it's natural to feel overwhelmed, have doubts, or have periods of waning motivation. When that happens, get outside of your head (a very helpful feminine aspect of leadership)! Get in touch—make a phone call to someone, take a trip to a museum, a bookstore, a favorite park, the beach, or even the mall; dance wildly and outrageously to unwind; meditate, or take a nap (It is amazing what just twenty-two minutes can do for your energy and your outlook.)

I don't know about you, but I spend a great deal of time in my head (my comfortable masculine-leading place). I am a planner, organizer, researcher, intellectual, and sometimes am more about doing than being. As I have studied leadership and put my own stamp on it with Comfluential Leadership, I've begun to spend more time in my heart where the feminine resides. It can be a place of rejuvenation, inspiration, calm, and creativity—all important parts of a successful movement or change effort.

What I have learned from the overwhelm that can occur is that I also need to be in my body, to really get in tune with the rhythms and changes going on continuously. When you disconnect your mind and heart from your body, havoc can occur. Find ways to bring yourself to truly BE in your body. I share some guidance on this in my book and workbook, *Awaken the Leader.*

Stopping, tapping into your feminine aspects, feeding your body, mind, and spirit with activities that inspire and nourish you—all go *a long way* towards keeping you inspired and motivated to create a movement that will make the change you so desire to happen. In doing so, you will get excited again and involve your team in the momentum of striving towards your goals and doing what needs to be done.

CHAPTER 7

Command vs. Influence

Y OU MIGHT STILL be asking yourself, What do command and influence have to do with each other, and why should I care? Both are really good questions.

For any woman with a vision to bring change to the world—be it running a socially conscious business, running an arts program in the schools, running for political office, or running her own home— *the distinction between leading through command and leading through influence is important.* We now know that command is my 'shorthand' for leading from the masculine, and you've gotten a good idea of what that looks like. Influence is my 'shorthand' for leading from the feminine. The core of influential leadership is to bring in our feminine strengths—the nurturing, compassionate, visionary creative qualities that will motivate and inspire a person to believe in your message and to WANT to follow you, as opposed to BE COMMANDED to follow you. Both have their place, and when a leader can blend these effectively, they are unstoppable! Let's go deeper . . .

"A Tiger Doesn't Lose Sleep Over the Opinion of the Sheep" (Shahir Zag)

When I started my career in the corporate arena, I found that men in leadership roles were very much like those in the military—telling me what to do, how to do it, and expecting me to just follow along. I was such a good student of command that I didn't know there was a different way of leading or influencing. While I didn't always comply without discussion or questions, I did learn my lessons well. In turn, in my leadership position as VP in banking I often used my command voice with my team.

Not surprisingly, I had a difficult time understanding why my team and I were never close. We had a more formal relationship like I had with my troops in the military. Because of the "no fraternization rules" between higher-ranking personnel and their subordinates, specifically enlisted and officers, I didn't think anything of it. It was what I also expected in a corporate hierarchy. Well, I was soon to learn another twist to this whole leadership thing.

I was one of very few women in a leadership position, and the corporate world of the masculine leadership model wasn't quite used to women leaders yet. We were expected to fit into that world, to be at least as competent as the men, and to hold our own in any situation. But, as I talked about earlier, when we mimicked our male models' command style, they became confused; this was not how women were supposed to act—too harsh, too aggressive, not ladylike!

Being commanding, focused, decisive, fearless—when these traits were displayed by a man, it was seen as a plus. When it exhibited by a woman . . . not so much.

Once I was even fired, despite the excellent work I produced! My boss told me there were two reasons: 1) He could never get ahold of me (I had a solution for that as I was in my car traveling for work most of the time: I suggested he get me a car phone); and 2) I was a mother and should be with my children and not working. In other words, I did not fit his model of a woman leader. (What possible solution could I offer for the fact that I had children?)

You might remember, or have heard about, Hillary Clinton's "baking cookies" quote back in 1992, in response to questions as to why she was deciding to practice law while her husband was governor of Arkansas. "I suppose I could have stayed home and baked cookies and had teas, but what I decided to do was fulfill my profession, which

I entered before my husband was in public life." It drew criticism from traditionalists who interpreted it as a dismissal of stay-at-home moms. But she went on to explain, "The work that I have done as a professional, a public advocate, has been aimed . . . to assure that women can make the choices, "whether it's full-time career, full-time motherhood, or some combination."[20]

Footnote: in 2016, Beyoncé performed at a rally for Hillary Clinton's candidacy for U.S. president and highlighted the quote on a giant screen behind her on stage. She said, "I want my daughter to grow up seeing a woman lead our country and know that her possibilities are limitless."[21]

When One Door Closes, Another Door Opens . . . on Planet Entrepreneur

Back to my journey . . . It was all too obvious to me that it was time to move out of corporate. So, I entered a new world which I like to call "Planet Entrepreneur." A different world for sure. No more were people jumping to attention, devoted to my command, standing when I entered the room, and getting things done ASAP! The familiar rank and rules no longer applied; my team was comprised of independent women, pursuing their own goals, in their own offices or homes, managing their own time and career and future.

I began to observe the feminine aspect of leadership and influence. However, it wasn't until most of my team had moved away from me—abandoned me—and my clients finished their contract without renewing that I realized I needed a different leadership mindset and model.

And what a great model it has become! I learned that **command is not true leadership.** I learned that people have their own dreams, visions, and goals, and that I can empower them to follow those dreams for themselves, rather than *command* them to follow mine without question. We work together for our similar visions to blend, so all our dreams can come true. I learned that this kind of compassion, openness, vulnerability, earnest empowerment, and guidance—this is the kind of leadership that brings people in, energized and excited to move together on their success journey.

As Bill Gates, founder of Microsoft, said in the nineties: "As we look ahead into the next century, leaders will be those who empower others." In today's world, true leadership has little to do with hierarchy, supreme authority, or command. Leadership is more about investing in people and trusting that they have the skills to do the work, and about collaborating with others to accomplish common goals. *There is an art and a science to these skills, and they can be learned.*

The Journey to Embracing Feminine Leadership and Influence

As I began to practice this type of leadership, I learned that the way to invest and trust in my team was to get to know the people—really get to know them. (You might imagine that this is NOT the way it was done in the military). This meant getting curious, asking questions, taking a sincere interest in who my team members were, what was important to them, and what they uniquely brought to the table; actively seeking their ideas and opinions, inviting collaboration, and not being afraid to develop deep relationships. As I talk about in Chapter 2, it means listening, truly listening, to what your people have to say. A colleague once said to me, "You have two ears and one mouth. Use them in proportion."

If you want to be truly followed, remember what your followers tell you. Sincerely ask them about it when you next get together. It will definitely up your leadership quotient. These are feminine qualities which never had a place in the masculine world in which I lived and worked. And I love it!

I learned how to listen, to provide a supportive ear for my people, and about personal as well as professional issues. As a leader, we're not there to 'solve' problems (that's not empowering); instead, we can be there to listen and provide positive, productive feedback. I incorporated into my culture the core value of *treating my team and my clients how they wanted to be treated—not how I wanted to treat them.*

Not only did my businesses turn around, but I found my true purpose—training and supporting women in leadership. I started a new career, and went on to write a book and develop a twelve-step system, both called *The Art of Herding Cats: Leading Teams of Leaders,* to train others how to become influential and extraordinary leaders as women.

The Feminine Side of Leadership Has Everything to Do with Influence

The core of the art and science of influential leadership is to recognize, and not hide, our feminine aspects. Bringing in the nurturing, compassionate, visionary qualities of the feminine will motivate and inspire the individuals to believe in your mission, to WANT to follow you, as opposed to being commanded to follow you.

When you believe in the value of something yourself, aren't you more apt to commit to action and see it through? It results not only in getting the job done, but also provides a much richer experience, don't you think?

As a woman in business, you may be keeping your emotions bottled up because you want to be seen as a professional. It's a natural thing to do. Believe me, I know! We women have been receiving that message for a long, long time. However, your team and your clients—and the world—need to see you being real. They benefit from seeing all of you, and success follows.

If you are someone whose experience is in the military or corporate world, or if you have buried your feminine leadership qualities a little too deep inside . . . then how do you begin to change the dynamic? Here is one way to start:

Move from your head to your heart. Influence comes from the heart; command from the head. You need both, of course, to be an effective leader. But too often we are so used to the traditional masculine model that we keep on analyzing and 'doing' when what we need in those moments is to tap into our heart: emotions, feelings, intuition, kindness, big picture, both broad and nuanced perspectives.

In order to understand the context of the feminine strength within you, it may help to have more insight into what brought you here historically, so you know where you have come from and how you can move forward with new, empowering knowledge.

CHAPTER 8

Gender Heritage: Women and Leadership

A S WOMEN, IT is so easy for us to fall back on our genetic and cultural heritage. We were once taught at a very young age that our role in life was to be supportive, to be "perfect," that we were less qualified than men to do jobs (typically related to anything technical, scientific, mathematical, business, or physical such as combat), that we were expected to "play by the rules," to prove ourselves by only applying for those jobs that we believed we were one hundred percent qualified for (before we even allowed ourselves to apply).[22] We were often told that the qualities that make us feminine were not valued, especially in the workplace or in politics. "Feminine" qualities include creativity, collaboration, cooperation, compassion, empathy, intuition, patience, vision, emotions, and "heart."

So, we hid them (and thereby, ourselves) behind a mask or behind a curtain. We were in the shadows.

Enter the Masculine Leadership Model . . .

If we did step out, it was by taking on the qualities of the masculine role model accepted by society, since men typified leadership. The "masculine" qualities included using our mind over our heart, process over vision, telling or commanding rather than asking, competing not collaborating, and being assertive or aggressive. However, when we exhibited these qualities we didn't fit the picture that men (and many women) had of what feminine is, so we became "*That* Boss!"— the woman who was disliked by men because she didn't fit the image they expected and by women because she appeared to have gone to the "dark side."

Why we are challenged with stepping into leadership? It's built into our genetic and cultural heritage. As young girls, we listened very closely to the wisdom of our elders, women especially. We were taught to be seen and not heard, even better was not to be seen at all, not to promote ourselves, to wait to be recognized, not to talk over others, especially men—and so much more.

When I was considering a career, the first advice I heard from almost every adult was that I should find a career from which I could step away when I married and had children; one I could return to when my children were grown. These careers include nursing, secretarial work, and, of course, teaching. These were the thoughts that were driven indelibly into my subconscious and which manifested as I grew older.

Let me offer other stories of gender heritage messages that might sound very much like your own . . .

Perfectionism

It was 4-H that really brought out my mom's need for me to be perfect. My project was to sew a skirt with a waistband and zipper, two of the more difficult things for a beginner to do. Each night we worked on the project. When it was complete, it looked amazing. I did not notice it at the time but as I look back, I realize that after I had gone to bed, my mom would rip out what I had done, and redo it. She was an excellent seamstress, so all was perfect. No one knew, including me.

This also showed up in my first knitting project. I chose a rather complicated sweater for a beginner, a cardigan with an intricate pattern on the front. When it was finished the stitches and the pattern were perfect, and of course I was pleased and proud of myself. Again, it was years later that it dawned on me that my mom had done the same thing here as with the skirt—taking over my project and learning experience to make it "perfect." I still have the sweater and I marvel at the workmanship even today while I realize what a (well-meaning) disservice she rendered me.

This, of course, has impacted the work I do and how well I do it. Often what happens is that I freeze, or I put off doing something if I don't feel I can do it perfectly. To ensure that I don't fail, I require a clear road map so I can know all the twists and turns before starting. I also follow the pattern, recipe, model, and such *to the letter*. Where is my creativity? I would say that it was torn out of me by perfectionism. I had the belief that making a mistake would definitely ruin someone's life. Ever felt this way?

To Be Hidden

Much of my life was spent finding a way to metaphorically and literally hide behind curtains so I could safely be unseen. Or to make myself seem invisible in a room of people. I used my need to be alone as an excuse for not mingling with people. While I was able to develop skills that used my ability to organize, bring structure to life, and support other more extroverted people to succeed, it was still hiding the other parts of me that could have been expressed (many, I know now, were feminine qualities which I believed were not of value). These skills also afforded me the ability to make myself indispensable in my job, which meant getting a promotion or another job was difficult, if not impossible. I was unconsciously doing everything I could NOT to be visible, not to excel, not to lead in my professional and personal life. This was truly my reluctant leader period.

It was also a time when I found in high-level meetings that my opinion did not matter. In fact, if the men in the room strongly objected to what I was saying or proposing, they would just interrupt and talk loudly over me—as if I weren't there speaking at all! At that time, I did not have the courage to tell them to "shut up" (or words to that effect), because I was brought up to be polite and "know my place." As I have come into my power as a leader, I've learned how to be heard effectively without annoying everyone and, more importantly, to accomplish what needs to be done. However, I have seen so many women in similar situations just curl up, sit down, and grow very small.

We can no longer allow this disrespect to continue. If we don't step out, step up, and step into leadership and let others know who we are and what we can do, we will never reach our vision and we will never see the changes in the world that are begging for us to take them on.

To Wait

We were taught not to ask, not to step outside our bounds, and to wait to be heard or to get an advancement in our position or a raise. "The biggest surprise for me when I became a manager was how many men asked for a raise, a promotion, or a bigger office. It came as a shock because I didn't ask for those things myself. Neither did the women I supervised," says Joanne Lipman in her 2018 book, *That's What She Said.* [23]

I once had a client who was frustrated by her lack of advancement. In fact, she had recently been let go because they didn't really know the value she brought to the organization. She didn't understand this and told me that she had regularly brought new project ideas to her boss, even including the outline of a plan. Her boss always told her how great the project plan looked, and that he wanted to look at it a bit more before he gave it the green light. The next thing she knew, her male colleague was given her project to run. She asked me, "How come?"

What was obvious to me was that she had never told her boss she was ready to take on a project manager role and wanted to manage these projects herself to show what she could do. She did not speak up. Men don't understand this type of behavior and tend to look instead to those who ask or are 'in their face.'

I gave her a suggestion: with her next boss, when she brought up a project, tell them that she wanted to be project manager. If it was felt that she was not ready yet, then request or accept being the sub-project manager so she could learn what was missing that she needed to learn.

The next step she took was to find a new job where she could start over with this new, more powerful mindset, which was great. However, she pored over job descriptions and if she did not know one hundred percent of the job, she would not apply.

She was a perfect example of what I talk about at the start of this chapter, how women tend to not apply for a position unless they believe they are one hundred percent qualified whereas men will apply if they know around sixty percent of the job.[24] They figure they can learn the rest on the job. We, as women, are afraid people will see us as frauds, something else we run from quickly due to heritage.

The Jobs

The other piece of "not asking" is that we have learned from other women as well as our own experience that you can ask, but there's a pretty good chance you won't get that promotion or new job, a conclusion that seems to be supported by research. A study published in 2018 found that "women do 'ask' just as often as men. They just don't 'get' . . . that, holding background factors constant, women ask for a raise just as often as men, but men are more likely to be successful. Women who asked obtained a raise 15% of the time, while men obtained a pay increase 20% of the time. While that may sound like a modest difference, over a lifetime it really adds up." [25]

In order to better understand why women face injustices in the workplace today, let's take a moment to look back at not-so-ancient history.

Gender Heritage: The Backstory

Back in the day, women did not work outside the home. They were the leaders of their household and, generally, they did not stray from there. If the home was on a farm, the woman was responsible for cleaning, cooking, childcare, and working on the farm either with the animals or in a kitchen garden. If the farm was small enough, she might even work in the fields. It was a sunrise-to-sunset-and-beyond type of job. If she wanted her own money, it usually came from selling something such as eggs, butter, and ribbons. Some women also took in laundry and sewing for extra money. All of this revolved around the home.

This changed as the United States became an industrialized country around the turn of the twentieth century. **Women began to work in the factories and offices** that were springing up in cities all over the country. Secretarial jobs became something one looked to as prestigious. A woman could move up from a pool secretary or a stenographer to an executive secretary working for a man in a top-level position with the company. In some respects, this hierarchy of secretarial work is still in place today.

My mom was an executive secretary to the top man at a research laboratory for a very large company. Not only did she have his work to do, but she also created the reports for the scientists. I was always amazed and in awe of what she did, and how fast she did it. She not only took dictation via shorthand, she also transcribed it, usually in triplicate, for her bosses' signatures. Unlike digital copy, if someone made even one change in a document, it usually meant having to retype the entire document, again in triplicate. It is truly easier today in so many ways!

Nursing was another field where women were finally accepted. Again, we did this throughout most of the wars and conflicts by treating wounded soldiers in our homes, hospitals, or on the battlefield. In fact, homes were often confiscated just for that purpose as well as for headquarters locations. Nursing schools were set up in hospitals where even my favorite childhood book character, Cherry Ames, was trained. It was only in the later part of the last century that nurses were educated in colleges and universities to gain not only their nursing credentials, but also college degrees. Today, nursing has created advanced degrees for the field. Even though nurses were once known to defer to doctors regarding patient care, nurses have been taking leadership roles in patient education and preventative care as well as the advocates for patients. We also now see women in Physician Assistant roles in which they have authority to take over some of a doctor's duties.

Teaching was another profession that became acceptable for

women to enter, since we had been naturally teaching our children at home long before home schooling became an alternative to public schooling, so it seemed to fit "our place" in society. Typically, it was an accepted position for young women before they were married because if they became pregnant, they lost their job. There were interesting rules to being a teacher, and this was one of them.

Women's roles in the military and during wartime have a storied history. I know how very heartbreaking it must have been for women during World War II who worked for the war effort in factories, airplanes, transportation, and offices, filling increased wartime demand or standing in for the men fighting at the front. When the war was over and the men returned from the front, these women were unceremoniously told that their services would no longer be needed. They were to go back home and go back to "keeping their place." During the war, we women held the crucial roles that kept the economy—and the war effort—going. We kept manufacturing running, maintained our families and social systems—even allowed to enter professional sports. (A wonderful depiction of this situation is found in the movie, *A League of Their Own.*)[26]

It was so very wrong. If we were good enough to do the job during the war, why were we not good enough after?

I've shared my story of job inequality which I experienced while serving in the U.S. Army. I continued to fight this injustice when I was in the U.S. Army Reserves. On one assignment, I was "double-slotted" as the Adjutant (staff officer who assists the commanding officer) with another officer, who was male. My boss told me in no uncertain terms that he did not respect women officers, that the fact that I was pregnant was repulsive to him, and that he would not give me any special treatment, but in fact would make my life miserable. Believe me, he did just that until my doctor told me the stress he was causing was harming the baby and I needed to make a choice. Unfortunately, I had to choose to leave the reserves rather than my civilian job.

Then there was the interesting situation in which I was recruited by several different units because of my outstanding record both while active and in the reserves (believe it or not). They wanted me as an assistant human resources and administrative officer. I asked what the rank was for the position; I was told it was a Captain's slot. Please understand I was a Major at the time, which ranks higher than Captain. I asked if the actual S-1 slot was open and was told yes.

So . . . why was I not considered for the position? Well, because they were reserving it for a male combat arms officer because he needed the reserve time, so he would be my boss. Needless to say, I turned them down because I knew what would happen: he would sit and shoot the bull, drinking whiskey and smoking cigars while I did all the work. He also would be the one to brief the Commander based on my work. This had been my boss-from-hell's modus operandi. I refused to put up with it again. I told them all, I would love to join their unit when they were ready to put me in the slot I was qualified for.

Let's Change the Story

If you are from the Baby Boomer generation, I'm sure you have your own stories just like mine about the challenging impact gender heritage has had on your life and work. To borrow from the 1968 slogan created for the Virginia Slims cigarette ad (the Philip Morris campaign wanted to cash in on the women's lib movement and targeted cigarette sales to women), "You've come a long way, baby."[27] And we have, I'm very happy to say. We are looking at the strides that have been made in women's leadership from the lens of the challenges we've faced.

If you don't identify as a Baby Boomer, I know you have stories to tell as well! We still have a long way to go to overcome our gender heritage in areas such as paycheck equity, positions in the C-Suite, safety from sexual assault and harassment, and opportunities without limitations.

CHAPTER 9

Leadership, Gender Heritage, and Money

WE CANNOT TALK about women, leadership, and gender heritage without including a discussion of women's relationship with money, past and present.

Money, prosperity, and I have had a checkered past. There have been periods of time when we were very close. I wooed and won money and prosperity into my life. We danced a beautiful, sensual Argentine tango and a bouncy salsa and a smooth, elegant waltz. Then there have been the times when it appeared that the dance with money and prosperity walked out of my life, leaving me with a huge hole in my heart of sadness and despair to wonder if the dance would ever happen again.

What I find interesting in looking back at those moments is this: ***when I am closely aligned with money and prosperity, my ability to lead is easy and effortless.*** It's because I am not in my head, but rather in my heart. When I am out of alignment—towards the masculine end of the spectrum—I worry about where and when the money is coming in, so far into my head working the numbers that I couldn't lead a horse to water much less lead a movement or business.

Our Relationship with Money

Why has my relationship with money been such a complicated one? Do you feel like yours has been, too? For many of us (male and female alike), money has always been an issue. It often wraps around our scarcity beliefs and thinking, developed over time for most of our lives.

For example, do any of these sayings about money ring a bell?

- Money doesn't grow on trees.
- Money is the root of all evil.
- A fool and his money will soon be parted.
- You have to work hard for money.
- It is not polite to take money from others.
- Neither a borrower nor a lender be.
- Time is money.
- Money can't buy you love or happiness.
- More month than money.

I grew up hearing every one of these. When you hear them, where does your mind go around money? Does it go to self-talk like this:

- "I don't have enough. I need more."
- "I can't afford it; it costs too much."
- "Is it on sale?"
- "If only I had the money, I could . . . "

Many of us grew up with parents, teachers, friends, and neighbors who stressed about money and talked about not being able to afford things that they wanted. Those messages became our thoughts and beliefs, recording in a continual loop in our heads. And they are so rooted in our subconscious that we often don't question them; we just live by them.

Even very wealthy individuals stress about money. Their worries may be different from those who are struggling to make ends meet, but I have never met a wealthy individual who feels they have "enough" and doesn't want more. If that were not the case then Oprah, Donald Trump, Bill Gates, and others would not continue to create the next new idea or business.

We are consumed by our lack of money. Even when we are successful, we are afraid of losing our success and stress about making that next payment, focusing on when the dance will stop, not appreciating the dance we've had or can make happen again soon. So, it isn't really about money as currency, is it? ***It's truly about our stories, beliefs, and thoughts about money and what it can or cannot bring us, along with what it does or does not represent to us.***

Our Gender Heritage Around Money

On top of these societal messages about money, we women can add the cultural messages and norms around money that have limited us. Women have always dealt with money, selling or trading eggs and vegetables from the farm, taking in sewing and laundry, managing dowries and properties, whatever was needed to take care of our families and interests. However, in most cases (even in today's world) they have not been given the power or authority to do so. It's no surprise that we women have received different messages about money than men have, which affect our relationship with money, leadership, and prosperity. Let's dive into a little history to help us understand why.

Egypt, c. 3100 BCE and after: Women held equal financial rights with men. "Egyptian women were able to acquire, to own, and to dispose of property (both real and personal) in their own name. They could enter into contracts in their own name; they could initiate civil court cases and could, likewise, be sued; they could serve as witnesses in court cases; they could serve on juries; and they could witness legal documents."[28]

Ancient Hinduism, c. 1500 BCE and after: Women had the right to control property before marriage, which included gifts from parents, friends, and strangers as well as earnings from her own work. Divorce was not allowed, and inheritance laws favored male family members.[29]

Ancient Rome: Freeborn Roman women were allowed to divorce, own property, and inherit from families (although preference was usually given to the first-born male).

In the Middle Ages, Islam allowed women the right to inherit estates, own property, and initiate divorce. Anglo-Saxon laws let women own their own property before and after marriage.

In Norse societies, women could conduct business as equals with men.

Women could own property–they weren't property. Then came the Dark Ages . . .

In the 1100s, English common law led to the creation of "coverture," the belief that married men and women were one financial entity. "As such, married women cannot own property, run taverns, or sue in court . . . Over time, coverture is corrupted into the view that women are property of their husbands."[30]

From that slippery slope, the Dark Ages and beyond became really dark for women in terms of limiting their actual financial independence and shaping beliefs that their value wasn't as high as men's, their place was in the home, they were "too fragile" for long hours or certain types of work, and other such lies.

Things began to change, slowly but surely. In America in the 1800s, laws began to be passed to allow women to have property in their own names. They were granted the right to file patents, and to become, for economic purposes, individuals—that is, *if they were still single.* In Mississippi in 1839, the Married Woman's Property Act (which thereafter quickly expanded to other states) strengthened women's claims to ownership and financial independence–ending centuries of "coverture" little by little.

Women began to take their place in financial management, entrepreneurialism, and knowledge of money matters—a few courageous pioneers at a time (and quite a few reluctant leaders who took the lead out of necessity). And, most significantly, women in their everyday lives, with the responsibilities of their households, managed their resources, made money, and invested it with an expertise that financial journalist Hartley Withers noted in 1930 was, "that wide-eyed skeptical curiosity that makes women so formidable."[31]

The societal messages persist to this day. Even though women are running their family households, businesses, international movements, and governments, for many there's still a discomfort with talking about money. I hear women say, "I was taught that it was impolite to talk about money." Or, "My dad handled all the money in my household, so my husband does now." Or, "Men are better with money than women—it's just always been that way."

Here are just a few lies you are being told by society:

- *You are not good at math and should not work with numbers.*

- *You are not good at financial matters; women are too emotional.*

- *You are bad negotiators, that's why you make less money than men do.*

Of course, we know that many of these myths are being busted every day. We also know that we CAN and MUST bring our "emotional" (feminine) side to our relationship with money, because money is about relationships—what money means to us and others, how it helps us lead our actions to our vision, how it offers creative ways that we can do the dance with money for our business and personal lives, and more.

The Scarcity Mindset

When we cloud our minds with stress and a scarcity mindset, we can't concentrate on attaining the necessary money. Instead we are sending a message to our subconscious to search the outside world for every possible way to reinforce the belief that we are in scarcity. Here is why: The subconscious mind is activating the Reticular Activating System (RAS), a bundle of nerves at our brainstem that filters out unnecessary information so the "important" stuff gets through. It's one of the wonders of brain function; however, the system's filtering basis isn't always to our advantage. If our subconscious is thinking scarcity and lack of money, then the RAS will scan for ways to NOT have the money arrive, or to find new ways to spend the money that we already have.

As you think, so the RAS makes it happen. If scarcity is your standard then that is what you will experience in your life. *Is that how you want to live your life? Or is abundance where you are going?*

In my work with women and their leadership, visions, businesses, and movements, I see how abundant thinking can become the norm, where the future is so vibrant that there is nothing else in the way. I find that when I am in scarcity thinking, it is difficult to think beyond the now to the vision of the future, and so easy to slide back into listening to those limiting messages we grew up with.

So, I choose and teach prosperity thinking in leadership.

Shift Scarcity Thinking to Prosperity Thinking

Here are some ways you can shift scarcity thinking to prosperity thinking by bringing in both your feminine and masculine strengths (Comfluential Leadership).

One way scarcity manifests is in spending money. Whether I was working in the corporate training world or the nonprofit world, if the goal was to "tighten the belt," the immediate go-to was to cut—people or programs or services to members. I can't tell you how many times I was asked as a corporate or nonprofit leader to cut items out of the budget, especially if the department was a cost center.

There is often this sense of scarcity involved, and it always seems to get to a point where there is nothing left to cut and it is still not enough. Like the body shutting down, eventually its core processes will stop working, and the death of the organism is the result. Wasn't there another way?

I learned that when the company was tightening its belt, it was time to have a prosperity mindset. It meant getting creative—as you remember, a feminine leadership quality. I did, of course, look at where we could be more efficient, but that was not all. My goal was to explore where we could increase revenue. For nonprofits, one way was to create events with paid advertising and which promoted more memberships, patrons, sponsors, etc. I also created initiatives that were benefits the members wanted so they would be excited to join or renew their memberships.

In the corporate training world, when I was asked to cut a dollar amount from my corporate budget I started with the trainings themselves: the cost of a seat in our workshops, and how many seats we needed. What was interesting was that if departments wanted more butts in seats, they paid for the privilege because they were revenue/ profit centers. They could actually sponsor an entire workshop just for their people. The revenue centers realized the value of the training. as we could show direct income increases and could compare it with the expense per participant. It was a huge success, a win-win for my department and for the company as a whole.

Another time, I got creative with employee salaries (a little more daring). I had a total dollar amount to cut just for the rest of the fiscal year. I could have let someone go and saved that money, but the following year's budget allowed me to replace that person. Going through letting someone go and rehiring in the new year didn't make sense to me (or probably to you either).

It was serendipity that I happened to be pregnant at the time and was due in September. With maternity leave, I was not due back until the beginning of the next year. What would you do if you had a prosperity mindset? That's right—I took myself off the payroll, thus saving the money out of my budget. The benefits to me were time to rest before the baby came, getting our home ready for the baby, and having the trainers in my department completely redefine the programs offered the following year. We all got the gift of time and space to create. Yes, I did come back the next year to a totally energized team ready to inspire our students in so many different ways.

If you ask people about the economy, those with a scarcity mindset will tell you all the things that are wrong with it and how it is in the tank for them. With a prosperity mindset, it is all about thinking outside the box and seeing the possibilities.

Which would you choose for the work you do? Scarcity thinking and always shrinking the organization? Or abundant thinking, looking for new and creative ways to expand?

Looking at Priorities: Where Is Your Money? When money and I are at odds, my father's saying about money haunts me: "If you want something, get it now as it won't be there when you come back!" For someone who under normal circumstances operates in her head, pondering key decisions long and hard, I need a rational process to make that happen. My dad taught me the "bankers' T" as a way of making decisions, which comes in very handy. (Send me a note and I will spell it out in detail for you.) Yes, my father's statement sounds less masculine than it does impulsive and emotional (feminine). Making more conscious buying decisions could be a perfect place to join together masculine and feminine. But more on that in the next chapter . . . meanwhile, here is an example for you:

In 2012, my family and I went through some significant changes. We downsized from a 3,700-square-foot house in which we had lived for eighteen years to a 973-square-foot apartment. Part of this move was due to the economy (money) and part was due to the fact that my husband and I were finally on our own with our daughters starting their own families.

In the process of moving I discovered something that would affect me deeply: My money was wrapped up in "stuff" rather than an investment in my retirement, my dreams, and my family. And, believe me, I had an incredible amount of stuff, such as . . . yarn.

My mother was a crafter. I felt so loved when my mom was knitting, needles clicking softly, the house quiet and calm. That was our time to talk and to go deeper in our relationship. I wanted that same environment for my daughters. So, I started knitting, too.

True to form, I developed the belief that if one project was good, then fifty was even better. I fell in love with the feel and look of knitting yarn and built a stash that could have started a knitting store! I would never get to it all, yet I kept expanding even further—money went into needlepoint canvases, cross-stitch patterns and kits, and fabric for quilting.

I hoped that my girls would catch the crafting bug, and that this would be our connection. Unfortunately, this did not happen. The girls were into dance and crafting for them usually happened in a class, not at home.

So why didn't I go solo and recreate the ambiance myself? The perfectionist in me reared its ugly head. I was afraid that I wasn't doing it right, and that it was not perfect. I hid my talent and only worked on projects when no one else was in the house. Because of this, none of the projects got done and the stash kept growing.

My aha! moment came when I had to gather all my crafting stuff for the estate sale. It was overwhelming to see all that I had accumulated and would never get to even if I lived to seven hundred and ten! It broke my heart to realize what I had done to our dreams by spending all that money. Our move would allow me a fresh start.

Nurturing a Prosperity Mindset

Today, I am more conscious of where my money is going. Stuff can't accumulate in the apartment as there is simply no room. I do a purge on each anniversary of our move to open up some space. I am also conscious of the fact that I'm paying off those excesses when I could be experiencing retirement or at least an increase in time to travel and build more incredible experiences. I need financial fluidity to handle this excessive debt. My prosperity mindset, with a closer relationship to money, has stepped in.

Another gift from this experience is that I am driven to help women grasp the concept I learned; how they may have sabotaged their dreams, and how they can turn it around. I am teaching them what I have learned so they don't have to make the same mistakes I did.

So, let me ask you: *Is your money in "stuff?" Or is it invested in the experiences you have built or are wanting to build?* Is your money helping you to create the extraordinary life you want to live and the dreams you want to see fulfilled?

This is what a prosperity mindset and a healthy relationship with money are all about. Both dance partners will support you in being an extraordinary leader as well as creating an extraordinary life.

CHAPTER 10

Comfluential Leadership

S O. LET US recap.

For hundreds of years of male-dominated leadership, men and women have received mixed messages about what leadership is, and who gets to be perceived and accepted as leaders. These messages have been ingrained in virtually every aspect of society's institutions in a way that favors command over influence, male traits and style over female, and men over women for leadership opportunities.

These biases run deep and often are unconscious in women as well as men. As we have seen, they are the foundation of practices that have limited women's potential for a very, very long time. And in doing so, this has limited the potential for a better world. On International Women's Day in March of 2019, His Holiness the fourteenth Dalai Lama tweeted: "Women have been shown to be more sensitive to others' suffering, whereas warriors celebrated for killing their opponents are almost always men. We need to see more women in leadership roles and more closely involved in education about compassion."[32]

It's time to heal the gender leadership rift.

Happily, times continue to change and awareness is growing about the value of *leadership characteristics which men and women both bring to the table.* As we're seeing more and more women step into leadership roles in corporate, government, and especially as entrepreneurs, it is the perfect time to heal the split between these two sides of leadership. And it's about time to fix those low percentages of women in CEO and Board of Directors positions as well as other positions of influence.

While neither the masculine nor the feminine model is the wrong way to lead, they are not complete; they are two parts of a valuable whole. What this means is that we need to heal the rift between them so that *each man and woman can become a truly influential leader.* We need Comfluential Leadership.

Remember, Comfluence™ is my term that "marries" Command and Influence to describe masculine vs. feminine leadership characteristics and styles. The most interesting and exciting part of this concept is this: **Each of us, male and female, possesses masculine and feminine traits.** I've described how I've lived much of my life tapping into my masculine, spending more time in my head than my heart and using command instead of influence, while of course I possess many positive feminine qualities. I just had to be reintroduced to them! While society has managed to put "male" and "female" into social categories (and stereotypes), that isn't the only way we function.

The first step in moving towards Comfluential Leadership is to recognize this truth about us humans, male and female alike: We each carry chromosomes of the other sex, and we each possess typical traits of the other sex in varying proportions. The challenge for each of us is to begin the exploration of who we are—FULLY—so we can leverage our strengths and superpowers and truly be the best people, and leaders, we can be.

I do want to point out that since my mission is to help empower women, I am speaking to them, but my sincere hope is for men to read this book and commit to stepping into THEIR own brand of Comfluential Leadership.

Where Can You Start?

In an executive education program out of Wharton University, called "Women in Leadership: Legacies, Opportunities and Challenges,"[33] women in business and influence are encouraged to be "exceptionally aware" of their own leadership styles and strengths in order to make an impact. Other important lessons for women that I've gleaned from this program: *1) to continually "build our strengths and skills so we can lead a variety of people," especially because the feminine includes that capacity for empathy; and 2) to be aware of and develop our masculine capabilities.* In so doing, we become empowered and powerful leaders! And we take part in changing old perceptions of what a leader is or should be.

The task for women is to embrace not only the qualities with which we are more comfortable but also to embrace our masculine side, about which we may be less familiar. This can be challenging— shifting behaviors we've known all our lives (or reclaiming those we've suppressed in order to fit in), moving out of our comfort zone, learning new skills. We may need to redefine or discover our own set of leadership qualities, drawing from those masculine and feminine aspects that resonate with and define us. The bonus is that we get to know ourselves more deeply than ever before, and can create a true leadership style that is uniquely and powerful OURS.

For those of us who have been groomed in the masculine leadership model, we may have to UNlearn some beliefs and behaviors, such as The Commander.

Understand "The Commander"

For myself and women who come from (and are still in) the military and corporate worlds, our healing challenge is to address The Commander we learned is the model of leadership. He gets things done. He asks minimal questions and just wants his orders to come down from the top. He really doesn't understand all this feminine stuff like getting the opinions of others on the team before making a decision, aligning everyone with the organization's vision, asking questions to ensure that everyone is on board with the plan and feels included, building relationships with the members of the team, getting into that personal stuff that doesn't really matter. Let's just get this done!!

For the woman who doesn't come from this background, The Commander can be very intimidating. He appears so strong, overpowering, take-charge, and can even come across as mean, uncompromising, and greedy. Where is there room for creativity, for collaboration? She needs him to execute the plan—if only she could get him to shut up and wait for her to do her thing, then they could be great work partners. As a result, she seldom enjoys turning projects over to him because she's sure he will ride roughshod right over her and not listen to a thing she says. This happens in the boardroom a lot! She is talked over by The Commanders in the room (male OR female), and usually ends up just shrinking back and hiding.

Command may work on the battlefield. As General Patton once famously said, "No good decision was ever made in a swivel chair." However, *there is no heart in command.* Command does not move someone to shift their opinion, take action, or cause change because they are inspired and believe in it—without force or coercion. In fact, I believe *many* good decisions can be made in a swivel chair, or rather, several swivel chairs around a table with a lively exchange of ideas, beliefs, creativity, respectful disagreement, and passion. **It's in this model that transformation - Comfluence™ - happens.**

As women learn to tap into their masculine side (a healthier, gentler version of The Commander, perhaps?), we will gain a better understanding of what it means as a leadership style, to identify it when it happens, know how to respond and, most importantly, choose the aspects we want to integrate into our own leadership model. We'll make mistakes; we'll judge each other . . . But let's be open about what is happening as the process of achieving Comfluential Leadership unfolds. These will be the times we'll want to call up our Influencer and show compassion and understanding towards ourselves and each other.

Embrace Your Feminine Side

Go ahead, don't be afraid! **Your masculine side is still there, available when you need it; you are not weak because you embrace your**

feminine! Welcome it into your relationships, make magic with it! Allow yourself to be curious, to ask questions, collaborate, cooperate, show empathy and compassion, be patient, and share yourself openly.

Recognize that the Masculine Side Completes You but Does Not Define You

Your masculine side is important: freedom, direction, focus, integrity, independence, confidence, action, and, yes, assertiveness. When you recognize and invite in your full self—masculine and feminine—you can see from the qualities I've been outlining throughout the book how influential and powerful you can be!

I'm grateful for my journey, my experience of seeing the more extreme aspects of leadership in action, in the military and in the corporate world during a period when women were just coming into their true power (and of course, we are still on that journey . . .). What I know today is that leadership exists on a spectrum—there are masculine and feminine ways to lead and to influence. One end of the spectrum isn't better than the other. In fact, the best leaders are those who marry the two into one, unique, empowered, extraordinary leader.

My hope and vision for all women is to honor YOUR unique brand of leadership, your own way of influencing others, tapping into all your natural feminine instincts to express your emotions, along with your natural masculine abilities to focus, get tasks done, and make confident decisions. Learning about and bringing out all of these amazing qualities—and the results you can see in making change—is an exciting and lifelong journey.

CHAPTER 11

How to Be a
Comfluential Leader

AS IN MOST areas of personal growth, we start with understanding and healing the past so we can step forward in the new direction we want to take with more freedom. It has taken centuries for the story of women to develop and our gender heritage to have become embedded in our cell memory. Things won't change overnight, of course—and I've told you I'm still learning and growing and probably always will—but here are my thoughts and steps you can take towards becoming the most powerful, influential, Comfluential, extraordinary leader you can be in every area of your life.

Face, Embrace, and Reframe Your Gender Heritage

First of all, we need to recognize it when it shows up. Like any thoughts that are ingrained in our subconscious, we have to untangle them. We bring the thought into the conscious and then look at the feelings which that thought brings up. Once we know this, then we can begin to change how we act, and not before.

This is truly the internal work that needs to be done before our actions will change our results.

Second, we need to acknowledge—and celebrate!—the leadership roles we have taken throughout history, no matter our "place" and how many odds. We have stepped up and stepped out to lead our families, communities, countries, and movements which has made the world a better place. Reluctantly or not, given authority or not, bending to or defying the male leadership model, given a narrow path or carving our own, women have a crucial place at the table of history. We need to claim it, every single day.

Third, we need to keep awareness of our story, of our power as women to lead in our businesses, our causes, our government, our lives. I've told you some of my story in the hope of teaching and inspiring you to tap into your leadership potential. As I have done, share your story with other women. Share what you have learned from this book and from your journey going forward. I would love to answer your post on Facebook, https://www.facebook.com/linda.patten.311, or for you to email me your story at linda@dare2leadwithlinda.com, or on my website www.dare2leadwithlinda.com.

We women are stronger together!

Improve Your Relationship with Money

"Around the world and in every U.S. state, women are more likely than men to live in poverty, with additional disparities by race/ethnicity, age, and education level. Despite a period of shrinking unemployment and strong job growth in many areas of the United States, negative developments such as slow wage gains, growing income inequality, and a weakened safety net have contributed to persistent and unacceptably high poverty rates, especially among Black, Hispanic, and Native American women and children."[33]

I believe that each one of us has a responsibility to take control of our relationship with money and our right to be prosperous. Having a scarcity mindset CAN be transformed into creating prosperity. Prosperity, like realizing a dream, is like a three-legged stool that needs these aspects to be balanced: *Vision, Structure, and Support.* **Let's defy gender heritage about money with a prosperity mindset!**

There are so many ways to make this happen. Here are just seven to spark your creativity (a valuable feminine leadership quality) and get you started:

1. ***Have appreciation for what you do have.*** Always be in gratitude. This is the Vision leg of the stool. Create a gratitude journal and record ten things you are grateful for each day, even on those days when it is tough to come up with them. It is a powerful motivator. If you don't have ten things you are grateful for in a day, then look at those things that you appreciate about you and your world. This can often be an even more enlightening part of the practice, as you might be looking at aspects you would like to see changed, AND you appreciate the opportunity to work on them.

2. ***Don't sweat the small stuff.*** Giving a bit extra can be a great way to transform your thinking. Several of the restaurants and online ordering sites with which I do business offer an option to 'round up' the change on your bill to the full dollar. This money is then donated to the business establishment's favorite charity. Other online retail sites, such as Amazon Smile, offer ways to donate a percentage of your purchase to a charity of your choice. These are easy, low-cost ways to feel prosperous.

3. ***Invite others to share in your good fortune.*** This action works on the Support leg, and could be a post on Facebook about something you have accomplished such as finishing a book, being on a radio show, bringing in a new client, or even taking a fantastic trip. Let others celebrate with you. This is critical to staying on track towards the prosperity you deserve, because good circulates more good.

4. ***Be willing to make and keep your commitments.*** When you keep your commitments and work from a place of integrity, you open up the floodgates to prosperity! Conversely, unresolved breaches of integrity can stop prosperity from

flowing. Do some journaling: write down anything that feels unresolved, jot down what you are feeling about that Then add the steps you will take to clear it up–and when. 'Clearing it up' may look like a simple phone call or a letter to the individual involved. It might be a deposit into their bank account through PayPal or Cash app. This is a way to begin the healing of this breach of integrity and get the prosperity flowing again.

5. *Add value in a relationship.* Bring your time and energy to your relationships to deepen connection and develop depth. Bonus: This will provide prosperity in other areas of your life beyond financial.

6. **Create a plan to get there.** See the possibilities and make a practical plan to follow. This is the Structure leg which makes the focus and determination possible. It provides a road map to where you are going on this journey.

7. *Stay focused on your vision.* See the future as you want to see it—the possibilities of something better, not all doom and gloom. I know that I sometimes get distracted which has me "chasing monkeys." Stick to the plan you created as it provides that focus and determination to see you through to manifest your vision.

These are just some of the many and varied ways to bring prosperity into your life. *In what ways will you step into your own intimate dance with money?* Bring that dance partner close, and relish all you can do to prosper as a Comfluential Leader!

Open Yourself to the Power of Knowledge

Take in the knowledge about leadership mindsets and skill sets that this book has offered. Practice and continue to learn. Pay attention to your feminine and masculine qualities, and continue to uncover them, own them, celebrate them, and leverage them.

As I have said, stepping into your unique Comfluential Leadership strengths and style will take courage. Another thing it will take is *vulnerability*—the power of allowing ourselves to be vulnerable, as Brené Brown says in her book, *The Power of Vulnerability: Teachings on Authenticity, Connection, and Courage.*[35] As I read her lessons on vulnerability, I'm struck by how in line they are with becoming an extraordinary Comfluential Leader. With deep respect for her work, here is my interpretation of these lessons for you to include in your practice:

1. **No more hiding our emotions!** When we repress our emotions in order to "stay calm," not look weak, be polite, or "behave," we are slowly killing important parts of who we are. It might make you feel uncomfortable and vulnerable to show your emotions, but take time to explore them, how you feel, how you express those emotions in front of your followers, team, or friends.

2. **"Vulnerability is not weakness. It's the most accurate measurement of courage,"** said Brené Brown in her viral TED Talk in 2010.[35] What I learned from my years in command is that, once I allowed myself to be vulnerable, so much opened up for me and I became more in touch with my authentic self. My life has become so much richer as a result.

3. **Show up, step up, and face your fears**. As you explore and share your feminine and masculine qualities, you WILL be criticized and there will be pushback (along with the upsides that are so worth it!). Just keep moving forward, and your courage muscle will get stronger and stronger.

4. **Strive for excellence, not perfection.** "The belief that if we live perfectly, look perfect, and act perfectly, we can avoid the pain of blame, judgment, and shame" is Brené's definition of perfectionism. And I am here to tell you, as a recovering perfectionist, that it doesn't work anyway! The perfectionist can be the most severe judge and shame-maker around.

I teach the idea of striving for excellence to be the very best you can be, whatever that looks like for you.

Masculine and feminine qualities and strengths in your unique combination–THAT's Comfluential Leadership!

5. **Dare greatly. Dare to lead.** "When we shut ourselves off from vulnerability, we distance ourselves from the experiences that bring purpose and meaning to our lives," writes Brené Brown in her book, *Daring Greatly*.[37] We women could choose to stay in our comfort zones, accepting our gender heritage, not making waves, giving up our dreams. Can you imagine that for yourself? I can't! That's why my company is called Dare2Lead with Linda, and is my life's work. So, take the dare to be vulnerable, opening yourself up to purpose and meaning beyond what you could ever imagine. Step into your Comfluential Leadership–and dare to lead!

Be Visible, Step In, Step Up, Step Out!

When I left corporate to land on "Planet Entrepreneur," it was a daring move AND I felt vulnerable. I had a lot to learn about leadership as an entrepreneur, as I've told you about in this book. As you recall, I was someone who hid behind the curtain and did not take credit for the work I had done, especially if it was outrageously successful (talk about avoiding vulnerability!).

Truly, I hid my leadership and my talent under a basket. When I think about that, I think of a garden. If I planted a beautiful flowering bush like a hydrangea and then put a basket or barrel over it, what do you think the result would be? Would it grow and flourish with those absolutely gorgeous blossoms, or would it wither and die because it had no sunlight and no nourishment? I was not taking my work out into the sunshine.

My business was withering and dying with no one knowing it even existed. That is not what I wanted. I wanted a practice that flourished with heart-based clients eager to step into leadership and create a movement that would change the fabric of this world.

So, my next step was to hire a coach to help me do this, and I found Success Coach Ann Evanston.[38] As you might recall earlier, this is where I proceeded to tell her the following:

1. I don't have a website.

2. I don't do blogs.

3. I don't do radio and TV, telesummits, teleseminars, or podcasts.

4. I won't write books.

5. I definitely don't do social media!

I had a huge vision for my business, but look at all the roadblocks I put up to block me from achieving it! Ann helped me realize that if I was not visible, this vision would not happen, and my dreams of prosperity would remain just dreams (the Structure and Support legs of the stool were very, very wobbly). I needed to be massively visible. I had to update my vision of me as a leadership expert.

So, what have I done to become visible? Here's a list of what my vision has accomplished as of Q4 2019:

- I'm actually in the third iteration of my website: www. dare2leadwithlinda.com. I love my latest edition as it represents my coming into my own Comfluential™ leadership.

- I have written close to two hundred blogs so far, and post on my website almost every week.

- I have hosted a radio show, now in syndication, called *Leadership Stars on Voice America*, and the guests that I interviewed are amazing leaders in so many different ways. My listenership extends throughout the United States, Asia, Europe, the Middle East, Africa, and Latin America. (It appears that the Arctic and Antarctica are not listening.) Check it out here.[39] I have been a guest on many other radio shows, podcasts, telesummits, and television.

- I have been a coauthor in, to date, six anthologies, four of which were #1best sellers or international best sellers. I have published *The Art of Herding Cats: Leading Teams of Leaders*, and, of course, this is my second independent book. Not bad for someone who was dead set against writing one book, much less eight! When I said I wouldn't write a book, I never thought of the world of magazines and digital media. I have been seen on ABC, CBS, NBC, Fox, and other digital outlets.

- Social media is still the bane of my existence, but I AM on Facebook and Twitter, and I have a private Facebook group for my program, *Leadership Inspiration*. I am so very grateful for my team, Kerry Hargraves and Bettyanne Green, who really make me shine in social media. I am getting better at posting, commenting, and sharing, and I have a way to grow here too.

  I am definitely NOT hiding now, and am loving every minute of it.

What does this mean to you, the Comfluential Leader? I am sharing to show that if a resistant person like me can learn to step up and into my fully potential as a leader—then so can you! When you step into visibility, potential clients and followers see you in all of these different ways, and recognize you and what you stand for. The donations, contributions, and just plain money follow. You can't grow a business or a movement from behind the curtain. You must be at the front of the stage leading visibly.

What Does It All REALLY Mean?

Comfluential Leadership is nothing less than a shift in the paradigm we have had on what leadership is for so, so many years. It is empowered leadership at its very best. It's the conversation starter to redefine what leadership is, to break through gender heritage. Tapping into our Comfluential Leadership abilities, *we women can truly change the world.* When you marry the masculine and feminine strengths that live within you into one unique, empowered, extraordinary leader, *you can't be stopped! And the world will change because of it.*

You may at this moment be thinking, "Well, that is all well and good; I'm interested." You may be saying, "I'm in! Thanks for the help to get started—but what's next? This feels a little daunting!"

Well, I have some ideas, skills, methods, plans, lots of heart, and some emotional intelligence to offer that will bring it alive. You have the "why"—would you like to know "how?" Then you'll want to look for my leadership training workbook, called *Awaken the Leader*, which includes skill-building exercises to do, to meditate on, to write about, to dance with, and to just enjoy.

Whatever you decide to do to step into your own brand of Comfluential Leadership, I ask you to . . .

Do it for your children.

Do it for your team.

Do it for your legacy.

Do it for the world.

CHAPTER 12

The Future of Leadership

THE GENERATIONS THAT follow are the future of leadership. We as leaders have the obligation to mentor, train, and be an example to them, to stretch ourselves in our Comfluential Leadership skills—the best of our masculine and feminine qualities—to really turn this world on its ear! To create the change that will bring about a better world, and to leave a legacy of the kind of sustainable success that Comfluential Leadership is capable of providing.

Thank you for coming along with me on this journey. I hope you see the art, science, and mission of leadership in a way you never did before, and you can see as I do how important taking a leadership role in your life is. Of course, not just any leadership, but Comfluential Leadership, which will bring out the best in you and, in so doing, bring out the very best in all of us.

I have some final thoughts and training for you, so let's dive in . . .

Mentoring the Millennials

It is probably obvious to you that I am a Baby Boomer, and proud of it. From Boomers to Millennials, there has been a great deal of change in the world. I find it interesting that change happens so fast that we have names for "generations" that look more like decades. For our discussion, I'm using the guidelines created by the Pew Research Center40 for the

Baby Boomers, born 1946-1964 (54-72 years old), and the Millennials: born 1981-1996 (22-37 years old).

We Boomers pushed for more equality in the workplace, in the home, in politics, and in finance. We have seen a lot—just in 1968-69 alone: the first humans landed on the moon, Woodstock Music Festival, the turbulent 1968 Democratic National Convention, the anti-Vietnam War march in Washington D.C, the Stonewall Riots for gay rights, the passing of the Civil Rights Act, color television, computers, and other enormous technological advances. We mourned the assassinations of Robert Kennedy, Martin Luther King, Jr., Black Panther Party members Fred Hampton and Mark Clark, among other public figures.

Millennials have had their own challenges, a generation that grew up experiencing: the 2001 World Trade Center bombing and its aftermath, the Gulf War, the Iraq War, Oklahoma City bombing, and the first of what has become a national epidemic of school and shopping mall mass murders. They came of age as the devastating recession and downturn of the economy in 2008 happened. Their early careers were impacted by the rising costs of a college education or the financial need to change majors in order to get a job, or struggles to find a job at all while competing with all the older men and women who had been downsized.

All in all, their careers may not be having the rapid rise that we Boomers expected at that age as our destiny. This is the boomerang generation, where many adult children move back with their parents, because either they couldn't find work or it wasn't enough to pay the rising cost of housing. They are living in the midst of the social upheaval of norms and injustice that are deep-seated and with backlashes in many unsettling, destructive, violent ways.

My experience as a Boomer feels much different from that of my two daughters of this generation and the other millennials I talk to. They seem to be on their own–they and their technology which, to me, can never replace real human contact, conversation, and relationships.

All through my teen and adult life I had mentors and role models who guided me through, teaching me "the ropes," training me in the knowledge I needed for my next career step, supporting me with encouraging words and a hug or handshake (most of these mentors were men or women in command mode, so not too many hugs!). Remember my swimming coach? I never would have achieved what I did without his personal support and guidance which far exceeded the pay he got for classes. Whatever form mentoring took, I'm very grateful for those individuals who were willing and able to mentor me.

In the years that I was in corporate human resources, there appeared to be career paths and natural progression in a person's discipline. I knew when I started the job in banking that I had a clear path up from a Compensation Analyst to a Vice President in human resources for Global Systems Services. I also did time in the training aspect and rose from a sales trainer to Vice President of Southern California Training.

Today, for millennials, this does not appear to be the case–advancement is not a given and career development often is not supported or considered company policy. As an individual, you're on your own; you are expected to watch the job openings or promotion notices and apply if you think you are qualified. Where are they getting the guidance to know how to look for the right college or training, to find the right job, or know how to request a raise? In my experience, it seems like many millennials don't know what it takes to make a succession plan or have a clear sense of what their work is really worth.

Sheryl Chamberlain, writing for Forbes.com, notes that millennials are "the first generation to be less well-off than their parents and facing obstacles such as limited job opportunities, soaring costs of living and student debt . . . millennials seem to have the odds stacked against them."[41] Yet, as I mentioned in Chapter 6, they as a group are the fastest-growing donor segment, and use innovative approaches to connect and shift towards a global, caring mindset. ***Millennials need our support!***

I pose these questions to you, and to us all:

Are we developing leaders who are able to build relationships, communicate effectively, and navigate their professional and personal journeys successfully?

Are we developing leaders who will carry on our legacies of growth, prosperity, and change for a better world?

Comfluential Leadership: Creating a Legacy

As leaders, what can we do? This is the time to begin to practice Comfluential Leadership. We as leaders need to bring in the influential side of leadership, especially empathy and compassion, and share it with the younger generations. There are myriad ways to do this in whatever walk of life we are taking leadership roles: military, corporate, nonprofit, community, and family level. Here are areas to consider:

1. **Are we modeling and teaching leadership?** If so, what kind of leadership? If we are going to get the qualities of influence into the model for leadership, we must begin to teach it as part of leadership development, not only in corporate training but also in school from grade school through advanced degrees as a topic that is mandatory at all levels.

2. **Are we providing feedback?** If we are not having real communication, then it is doubtful that true feedback is being shared in both directions. There are so many ways to give and receive feedback, yet I believe people are afraid to do so. There is the fear that it will be taken the wrong way and could actually lead to lawsuits. I learned the "split feedback" method–tell them something good, then something bad, then end with something good. What do they remember? The something bad. Personally, I use the "liked best/next time" method with a twist.

    When critiquing sales trainees, I wanted them to focus on what they had done well first. After the sales call, I asked them what they liked best about the call and what they thought they had done well. (It is easy to beat yourself up after a sales call.) I wanted them to remember the good areas immediately. It gave them confidence and a sense of accomplishment. I always had a quick strategy session with the trainee just before the next call. At that time, I would say, "On this call, let's work on summarizing the call before asking for the business" or words to that effect. Now they had the opportunity to do something with the feedback right then. It worked like a charm.

The key here is if a person is going to grow and master the job, they need feedback to keep on track to success. We need to acknowledge people whenever we can. It is a way to foster motivation within.

3. **Using the team** is one of the key steps in my work on *The Art of Herding Cats: Leading Teams of Leaders.* This is where having deep relationships is so vital. What are the strengths and areas to work on in your team members (whatever their age)? Knowing this allows you to assign projects and plan training. Give them the opportunity to fail as well as succeed, as both are important for growth. Something else that is important in using the team is helping members with their people skills. Connecting as much as humanly possible by reducing the emails, making more phone calls (sometimes you get more done that way anyway), and personally stopping by someone's office or cubicle or chatting in the hall–not to check up on them, but to ask a question or make a light, positive remark. By the way, this is also a great way to help build self-confidence and expand people's sense of value.

4. **Find or be a mentor.** When I was in corporate, I carefully chose my mentors. Again, they were generally men, often considerably older than I was and with the experience that I needed for the next level. Later, when I started my business I looked for successful entrepreneurs to mentor me in that journey. With the pace of business these days, mentorship often takes a back seat, so it may take a little longer or more ingenuity to find the right mentor, but it's worth it!

Here are some tips on mentoring relationships: a mentorship is a two-way street, and it is a contract even though no money is exchanged. The agreement is not indefinite, and either party can end it when it feels like it is no longer serving them. Each party in the arrangement needs to agree on what each gets from the mentorship. The mentor might be looking for a better understanding of the mentee and that generation. The mentee is usually looking for experience, growth, and learning for the next job opportunity.

It is important that the mentor not be afraid to share her failures along with her successes. Becoming a goddess on a pedestal can often lead to a fall from grace when your failures are discovered. Share them in the context of learning from them, not just airing dirty laundry. Just to be clear, mentors always have time for their mentees!

Comfluential Leadership for a better world

The future of leadership is in our hands. We can choose to remain entrenched in the old masculine model of command and sit in our ivory towers bemoaning the fate of the world when the next generation is in power. Or, we can embrace the marriage of the masculine and feminine models and truly use Comfluential Leadership to bring the new generations into a changed world.

We can work towards a world without greed, war, terrorism, pollution, lack of safety for humans and animals, hunger, human suffering in all its different aspects and more, or we can stick our heads in the sand and hide from it all, waiting for the world to disintegrate.

Endnote

FROM MY EXPERIENCE–AND what I have come to believe–when we embrace and practice Comfluential Leadership, when we create a leadership style and essence that brings out who we truly are, soon it becomes a part of us. We just ARE–not our gender heritage, not fitting into an image of the stories we've heard, not defying odds against us, not coming from scarcity or fear. Just leading.

For any woman with a vision to bring success to her business or change to the world, run for political office or run an arts program in the schools, being a Comfluential leader is very, very powerful.

Let's imagine this together.

What would it be like to build a movement or business with leadership that comes from a place of wholeness? What kind of success can you picture when you build from this place rather than through separation, confusion, scarcity?

Well, when we use Comfluential Leadership, we begin to change the very fabric of our world for the better. We bring people in, they willingly come along on our journey, and we are joined together in the same passion, motivation, and vision, which is a powerful formula for sustained success and legacy. Like making a patchwork quilt, each piece contributes to make one beautiful, lasting whole–command and influence, action and visioning, analytic thinking and intuition, competition and collaboration, reasoning and relationships, calculation and creativity, assertion and connection.

When we bring the two sides together in agreement, the dance that they can do together is magical. There is true fluidity to it. "She" creates, aligns, and builds electric connections; "he" executes with precision and brings the team along with him. Imagine a beautiful Viennese Waltz, where both partners know their role and create that inspired moment on the dance floor. What it means for the movement and your business is that the connections and clients you need come to you with ease. They are attracted to the energy of the work that you do and want to be a part of it. Isn't that magical?

Now is the time to step in, step up, and be courageous–Dare2Lead!!

References

Introduction

1. "The Master List of Women in Combat." Rejected Princesses. https://www.rejectedprincesses.com/women-in-combat

2. Davidson, Renee. "Why We Need to Stop Equating Leadership with Masculinity." AAUW. Mar. 18, 2016 https://www.aauw.org/2016/03/18/masculinity-isnt-leadership/

3. "The State of the Gender Pay Gap 2019." PayScale. https://www.payscale.com/data/gender-pay-gap

4. Forbes Coaches Council. "15 Biggest Challenges Women Leaders Face And How To Overcome Them." Forbes.com. Feb. 26,2018.

5. McGregor, Jena. "Women make up just 11 percent of the highest paid jobs in corporate America." Washington Post. May 3, 2018.

6. "The Command Voice." Army Study Guide. ArmyStudyGuide.com. https://www.armystudyguide.com/content/army_board_study_guide_topics/drill_and_ceremony/the-command-voice.shtml

Chapter 1: This Is Me

7. "You Must Be Fit." Physical Training, War Department W.A.C. Field Manual. U.S. Government Printing Office. 1943

Chapter 2: Leadership: What It Is and What It Is Not

8. Coffelt, Sherri. "The Rule of 3." Results Partner Business Coaching/Consulting. https://www.resultspartner.com/

9. Goleman, Daniel. "The Focused Leader." Harvard Business Review. December 2013.

10. Nicoll, Bob, MA. *Remember the Ice and Other Paradigm Shifts.* Remember the Ice LLC, Publishers. 2008

11. Goudreau, Jenna. "Billionaire Spanx founder Sara Blakely shares her best business advice." Business Insider. Jan. 16, 2015.

Chapter 4: Leadership and Management: Not the Same Thing

12. Bennis, Warren. *On Becoming a Leader.* Basic Books. 2009

13. "Leadership vs. Management." ChangingMinds.org. http://changingminds.org/disciplines/leadership/articles/manager_leader.htm

14. Nayar, Vineet. "Three Differences Between Managers and Leaders." Harvard Business Review. Aug. 2, 2003.

Chapter 5: The Reluctant Leader

15. Vassolo, Martin. "Parkland students who became activists after massacre just won a prestigious global prize." Miami Herald. Nov. 20, 2018.

Chapter 6: Change Agents and Movements

16. Merriam-Webster Dictionary. "referenced word." Accessed August 2019.

17. Rafferty, John P. *Women's March.* Encyclopaedia Britannica. https://www.britannica.com/event/Womens-March-2017

18. Chamberlain, Sheryl. "Millennials Are Geared Up To Create Impactful Change I The Nonprofit Sector." Forbes.com. Jan. 11, 2018.

19. Salerno, Ann and Lillie Brock. *The Change Cycle: How People Can Survive and Thrive in Organizational Change.*

Chapter 7: Command vs. Influence

20. Nicks, Denver. "This was the Hillary Clinton Comment That Sparked Lean Dunham's Political Awareness." Time.com. Sept. 29, 2015. https://time.com/4054623/clinton-dunham-tea-cookies/

21. Reilly, Katie. "Beyonce Reclaims Hillary Clinton's 'Baked Cookies' Comment at Rally." Time.com. Nov. 5, 2016. https://time.com/4559565/hillary-clinton-beyonce-cookies-teas-comment/

Chapter 8: Gender Heritage: Women and Leadership

22. Lipman, Joanne. *That's What She Said: What Men and Women Need To Know About Working Together.* HarperCollins Publishers, 2018.

23. Lipman, Joanne. "Women are still not asking for pay rises. Here's why." World Economic Forum. Apr. 12, 2018.

24. Mohr, Tara Sophia. "Why Women Don't Apply for Jobs Unless They're 100% Qualified." Harvard Business Review. Aug. 25, 2014.

25. Artz, Benjamin, Amanda Goodall, and Andrew J. Oswald. "Research: Women Ask for Raises as Often as Men, but Are Less Likely to Get Them." Harvard Business Review. June 25, 2018.

26. *A League of Their Own.* Directed by Penny Marshall. Columbia Pictures. July 1, 1992

27. "You've Come A Long Way, Baby: Virginia Slims Advertising Year By Year." Flashbak.com. https://flashbak.com/youve-come-a-long-way-baby-virginia-slims-advertising-year-by-year-365664/

Chapter 9: Leadership, Women, and Money

28. Johnson, Janet H. "Women's Legal Rights in Ancient Egypt." Fathom Archive. http://fathom.lib.uchicago.edu/1/777777190170/

29. McGee, Suzanne and Heidi Moore. "Women's rights and their money: a timeline from Cleopatra to Lilly Ledbetter." The Guardian.com. Aug. 11, 2014.

30. McGee and Moore. "Women's rights and their money."

31. Withers, Hartley. *The Quick Sands of the City and a Way Through for Investors.* AbeBooks UK.1930.

Chapter 10: Comfluential Leadership

32. The Honorable Dalai Lama. "Tweet Message." #International WomensDay. Mar. 8, 2019.

33. "Women in Leadership: Legacies, Opportunities and Challenges" Executive Education Program. Wharton University. June 13-17, 2005.

Chapter 11: How to be a Comfluential Leader

34. "Poverty & the Social Safety Net." Institute for Women's Policy Research. 2019. https://iwpr.org/issue/poverty-welfare-income-security/poverty/

35. Brown, Brené. *Power of Vulnerability: Teachings on Authenticity, Connection and Courage.* Sounds True, Boulder, CO. 2012.

36. Brown, Brené. "The Power of Vulnerability." TEDxHouston https://www.ted.com/talks/brene_brown_on_vulnerability?language=en

37. Brown, Brené. *Daring Greatly: How the Courage to Be Vulnerable Transforms the Way We Live, Love, Parent and Lead.* Penguin Random House. 2013.

38. Evanston, Ann. Success Coach. http://www.warrior-preneur.com/

39. Patten, Linda. "Leadership Stars." VoiceAmerica Empowerment Channel. https://www.voiceamerica.com/show/2616/leadership-stars

Chapter 12: The Future of Leadership

40. Cripe, Katie. "Which Generation Are You? Pew Research Sets Guidelines." Pew Research Center. 2017.

41. Chamberlain, Sheryl. "Millennials Are Geared Up To Create Impactful Change I The Nonprofit Sector." Forbes.com. Jan. 11, 2018.

Acknowledgments

WHEN YOU WRITE an acknowledgment, you are telling the world that without these people the book would not have been written. There are many people who fit this category for my book. Let me take this space to recognize them.

First of all is Bettyanne Green, a writer in her own expertise and my editor. Without her this book would not have had the perfect elements in the perfect order. Her work on this book went way beyond what I ever imagined I could have. Thank you, Bettyanne, for being willing and extraordinary in making this book a reality.

This second person has been an integral part of my work for a long time. Kerry Hargraves is my integrator and keeps my work on time, on purpose, and beautifully rendered. It was her artistic talent that brought the cover to life, and her honest feedback helped the book move along. Sometimes I can ask for outrageous things of Kerry, and she has always been willing to learn it or just plain make it happen. Thank you, Kerry, for being the creative genius you are.

Then there is the woman who has been in my life for a long time. I am proud to call her friend, as well as the driving force in getting this book promoted around the world: Rebecca Hall Gruyter.

Thank you also to all the reviewers for your words of recognition. Your thoughtful comments brought tears to my eyes and gratitude to my heart. Many thanks to my forward writer, CJ Scarlet, who has followed much of the same path as I. Her books to protect our daughters and ourselves are guidebooks that every girl should have on her bookshelf—heavily underlined and well used.

Finally, I would like to thank my family—my husband, my two daughters, their husbands, and my granddaughter for their continued loving support in all that I do. Just know that I felt your support every day of this project. You cheered me on when the going got rough. You inspired me to be my best.

Enjoyed what you just read?

Please take a second to leave a review. We value your feedback.

A Sneak Preview of
Awaken the Leader
by Linda Patten . . .

Chapter 1

Awaken the Leader

N<small>O</small> O<small>NE</small> S<small>TOOD</small> *Up When I Entered the Room: One Woman's Journey from Command to True Leadership* was written as a guide to all the aspects of leadership. It started out to be a book about all the steps to growing a movement while moving into your Comfluential Leadership. However, as I wrote, I kept thinking about how someone would make the shift into leadership, with all its history, aspects, styles, and skill sets. I found that the two parts of the book did not go together. One was about my story and how I moved from command to Comfluential Leadership (and what that actually is); the other was the recipe on how to do it—the two were not mixing well.

Thus, *No One Stood Up* proceeded to take on a life of its own, looking deeply into leadership and its aspects. It soon became obvious that a second book would be needed to cover the concept of movements that create lasting global change, and to walk you through what it takes to accomplish each of the steps in growing a movement. That is how the subjects of the books were conceived, and how they were and are being written.

What I will be giving you in this book revolves around my teaching style, which is describing the "what," "why," "how," "example," and real-world practice. We will explore the following aspects of a movement:

1. **The Leader**—While we have done a great job of defining the leader, it is important for you to know how you step into that leadership. How do you balance the feminine qualities with the masculine qualities to truly become that Comfluential leader? How do you bring the feminine forward with the masculine watching her back? It is a powerful dance that is being done to create the special kind of leader it takes to lead any significant change effort.

2. **The Movement**—What is a movement? What does it mean to you? We will look at what your movement is and where it has been hiding all these years. This is truly the cornerstone of the change you will make. Without this clear definition, nothing will change.

3. **The Vision**—Everyone, every business, and every movement requires a clean, clear, and comprehensive vision. This is the feminine side of leadership, being able to see the big picture and visualize the dream. It must incorporate all of your senses in order to have your unconscious work to make it realized. Here we set your destination so that you can look at how you will get there.

4. **The Milestones**—Every vision and project needs goals and milestones. These are the aspects that move you towards the end result. The milestones are the big results and the goals when combined produce those big results. This is the masculine side of working on your vision. It provides the structure to it.

5. **The Connections**—For every movement, people are needed. How do you identify and find those electric connections and allies that will provide you with sponsorship, donations, supporters, collaborators, and followers? How do you develop and connect with personal as well as business connections?

What are the skills needed to build and maintain deep relationships?

6. **The Time**—Finding time is always a challenge in our busy lives. We feel that we have just enough time for our business, our family, and sometimes even ourselves. What usually goes first is the time for self-care and rejuvenation. How do you find the time to add the movement into your life? How do you manage the choices you make, not the time you have? Why are rituals important in managing your time?

7. **The Message**—How will the world know about your movement if you are not out there, visible and talking about it? How do you craft a beautiful three-minute speech that has your audience asking for more? How do you get excited about standing on your soapbox and projecting to everyone around what you stand for and what change you want in the world?

At the end of the book, you will have the steps, strategies, and details you need to actually stride into your own movement that will change the world as we know it.

Congratulations on taking this journey into the unknown. I'm beside you all the way . . .

About Linda Patten

L INDA PATTEN, Leadership Expert, Trainer and Mentor, is on a mission to do nothing less than fundamentally change how leadership is done in the world! Through Comfluential Leadership, she helps women and men leverage both the masculine and feminine strengths that live within, and dare to become the skilled, fully expressed, extraordinary leaders that they were always meant to be.

With 40 years of leadership experience spanning the military, corporate, and entrepreneurial arenas, Linda is uniquely qualified to guide women on their journey of self-discovery, skills development, and a charted course toward becoming effective leaders. Linda's business, Dare2Lead With Linda, *Awaken the Leader* trainings, and *The Art of Herding Cats: Leading Teams of Leaders* book and 12-step leadership program, are rooted in her heartfelt vision of empowering women to step out, step up, and step into the kind of leadership that creates positive change in the world.

Linda is known for her high-caliber interactive keynotes and trainings, and as the popular host of her syndicated VoiceAmerica radio show, "Leadership Stars." She holds an MBA in Organizational Behavior and Leadership, a Certificate in Meeting Management, as well as leadership positions in numerous professional management associations and women's business networking groups. Linda lives in the San Francisco Bay Area with her husband Clark and dog Connor.

Linda Patten
Leadership Trainer for Women Entrepreneurs and Changemakers
Dare2Lead With Linda
1250-I Newell Avenue #240
Walnut Creek, CA 94596
Tel: 925-954-3239
Fax: 925-258-9569

Praise for

No One Stood Up
When I Entered the Room:
One Woman's Journey from Command to True Leadership

"Linda Patten's book focuses on the positive actions that bridge the gap between the difficult realities of leading in this negative world and the inspiring possibilities of how leadership can redefine those realities for positive transformation. Linda refers to a significant dynamic of this reality redefining as Comfluential™ Leadership: bringing out the feminine and masculine strengths that are in  us so we more fully express as powerful leaders. Today's challenges require a redefinition of long-standing stereotypes of male leadership styles to insure we Work Positive and collaborate more productively. As a former Army officer and C-suite leader, Linda is uniquely qualified to help us learn how to redefine the current work reality and achieve our business dreams."

—Dr. Joey Faucette
Executive Coach and Author of two #1 Best-Sellers including
Work Positive in a Negative World
http://GetPositive.Today

"Whether you have been leading for one year or 20 years, this is a must-read book for all women leaders. Linda spreads light on how women leaders can use their unique talents to command and influence their team members to greater levels of productivity. Both insightful and practical, Linda's wisdom supports your growth to the next level of leadership."

—Sherry Winn
CEO/Founder The Winning Leadership Company
www.TheWinningLeadershipCompany.com

"Brava, Linda Patten! This masterpiece on (re-)creating one's self as the truest of leaders deserves a place on every women's studies/ business leadership course syllabus and woman's bookshelf! It is the perfect blend of solid observation of the traditional approach to women's leadership, the way(s) in which women *should* be approaching life as leaders (regardless of where that may be—the corporate world, home,

school, etc.), and insightful advice on achieving this 'new' and whole way of operating by blending our feminine and masculine abilities, traits, and leadership style approaches. By generously peppering the text with examples of her own lived experience, Linda also invites us to journey with her, sharing in her own personal story of realization, acknowledgment, acceptance, and actualization of the power of her feminine leadership abilities, allowing them to emerge from behind the curtains of societal conditioning and expectations. And, with gentle firmness, she dares the reader to do the same."

Nancy Tarr Hart, PhD
https://walkinginwisdom.life   tarrheart@gmail.com
https://www.facebook.com/nancy.t.hart.9
https://www.facebook.com/Wisdoms-Daughters-1189457091202840/

"A must-read for any woman (or man— if he dares) to journey through some history of women (and men) and the evolution of leadership from Command to Influence, which Linda Patten has coined "Comfluence™." Leadership is a balance between doing and being, and Linda provides not only inspiration, but

also the mindset and practical skills for all of us to lead 'extraordinarily.' A powerful book with compassionate wisdom from a former Army Major to a phenomenal Leadership Trainer for Women Entrepreneurs and Changemakers. A thought-provoking, empowering and transformative book."

Kimberly Schehrer, PhD
Bestselling author of *Unstoppable Teens*
Teen Breakthrough Expert and CEO of Academy for
Independence www.AFI4Me.com

"Linda's dynamic book: No One Stood Up When I Entered the Room is an insightful and empowering book that helps all of us more fully and effectively step into our leadership. Linda has expanded the definition of leadership to bring together the masculine and feminine styles of leadership to truly form a powerful way to lead with confidence, courage, and heart."

Rebecca Hall Gruyter, Global Influencer
Founder/Owner of Your Purpose Driven Practice
CEO of RHG Media Productions
Top Professional Quoted on: ABC, CBS, NBC & Fox
#1 International Best Selling Author, Speaker,
Publisher, TV & Radio Show Host/Producer,
and Empowerment Leader

"There's so much I loved about Linda Patten's inspiring book, beginning with her brilliant leadership concept COMFLUENCE™! Linda has created a wonderful container for women and men to finally begin blending the best of both genders' natural talents and strengths, into a leadership model that finally bridges our hopes and dreams into a  force for good in the world. I am so excited for this book to reach the hands of readers. Whether you're a female leader or aspiring to be one, you'll find Linda's book specifically meant and written for you! Linda unlocks the mystery of what it takes to be a supremely successful leader in the 21st century. Her unique military and corporate leadership background, rich wisdom, powerful storytelling, practical strategies and valuable reflective questions, make this an essential resource for women (and men) ready to courageously lead. Thank you, Linda, from the bottom of my comfluential heart!"

Marlene Elizabeth
Spiritual Life Coach For Female Leaders Treasured &
Transformed™ www.marleneelizabeth.com

"As an educator and fellow leadership expert, I found Linda Patten's book to be an invaluable resource for any woman or man who wants to understand leadership in a whole 'holistic' new way. Her timeline of women's leadership through history is a story that every young woman should read. How we got to where we are today in terms of leadership informs and inspires us to be more powerful leaders in the future. This book not only presents this perspective in a thorough and  even-handed way, it also goes further to offer practical insights and tips to help make influential leadership a reality. Linda brings her points to life with her own enjoyable stories of actualization to become a 'comfluent' leader, one who embraces and leverages both the masculine and feminine strengths each one of us possesses. I learned, I laughed, I was inspired, and I enthusiastically want to share this important book to all the women I know so they can be the strong leaders who will take us into a bright future."

Maureen Metcalf
Founder, CEO, and Board Chair of
the Innovative Leadership Institute
https://www.innovativeleadershipinstitute.com/

"This book is an open letter to the leaders in all industries who are ready to step into effective leadership—regardless of gender. This is THE defining book on leadership of our age. When you read *No One Stood Up When I Walked Into The Room*, you'll learn how to influence without convincing; command without controlling; and to start leading through comfluence, perfectly blending influence and command—to create  a brand-new leadership technique that is sure to transform the way leaders lead in every industry."

Cory J Center
Co-Founder with Becky Center,
School of Mystic Arts (SOMA)
www.SchoolOfMysticArts.com
Admin@SchoolOfMysticArts.com

Moving in the direction of feminine leadership is crucial in our ever-changing world and yet it is still only half of the story. Comfluential Leadership perfectly captures the dance between the masculine and feminine and is the necessary handbook for the next generation of leaders. We need true leadership now more than ever; leaders who create value, inspire  growth and influence the direction of their teams large and small. No One Stood Up is a testament of the call to the leader within, whether a reluctant one or not. Heed the call, take a stand for yourself, for your family, your organization, and our global community as a Comfluential Leader.

Becky Center
Co-Founder at the School of Mystic Arts
info@schoolofmysticarts.com

"No One Stood Up When I Entered the Room is insightful and groundbreaking. Having navigated the good, bad, and ugly of corporate America in the 80s as one of few women in the boys club I was playing in, the book brought up many memories of how early in my career, I stuffed down my natural inclinations  (female leadership characteristics) to fit in with the corporate norm.

Even as I "bucked the system" and created my own style, gaining the nickname "the Velvet Hammer" (because I got things done, but in a way that was collaborative and had people want to create the results), most of the men in my organization just didn't know what to do with me!

For today's female millennials and baby boomers alike, this book is a must read to understand the history of how women got to where we are today in business and leadership, and a lot about what's held us back from fully expressing our true brilliance. Perhaps more importantly, Comfluential Leadership provides a framework for shifting towards leading like only women can, which will change the face of leadership, and our world, forever."

Sherri Coffelt
Founder and CEO
Results Partner Business Coaching/Consulting
www.ResultsPartner.com

"Linda's work is a profound example of the shift that *must* happen in leadership today! Her research, experience and wisdom are essential for any woman who wants to embody a 'fully-expressed leadership style' in today's world. The blending of command and influence—Comfluence—is what is necessary to make the changes imperative to our future. This is a must-read for women everywhere *since all women are leaders.*"

Victoria Buckmann
Sales Magic Trainer, Wealth Genius Mindset Mentor Sales Magic Inc.
http://programmedforwealth.com/
925 399 2649
Victoria.Buckmann@gmail.com

"Thank you, Linda Patten, for writing a totally relatable book that inspires all women to step into their leadership power—not the old tired masculine model but a new model that integrates the best of the feminine with the best of the masculine. We only wish this were required reading for women of all ages and backgrounds! As the Dalai Lama said, 'The world will be saved by the western woman.' It's time to get on with it and this book is a great guide!"

Aimée Lyndon-Adams & Karen Renée Halseth
Co-Founders, What Truly Matters: Living Life Consciously:
www.whattrulymatters.com   info@whattrulymatters.com

"I loved how Linda Patten weaves her story and perspective into this informative leadership guide on how to be a well-balanced leader. The term Comfluence™ is sure to catch on. This book certainly inspires me to lead!"

Aeriol Ascher, MsD.
Healing Body Mind and Soul Podcast Host
Author, Speaker, Mentor, Coach
askaeriol@aeriolascher.com
www.somasoundtherapy.com
www.aeriolascher.com

Made in the USA
San Bernardino, CA
06 January 2020